BENDING PALMS

A MOTHER AND DAUGHTER SHARE
THEIR STORIES OF FAITH,
RESILIENCE, AND THE MIRACLE
THAT CHANGED EVERYTHING

By

TRISHA F. ESPINOZA
& TONI F. ESPINOZA

FLOWER POP PRESS
AUSTIN, TEXAS

FLOWER POP

Copyright © 2024 by Trisha F. Espinoza. All rights reserved.

Published by Flower Pop Press, Austin, Texas.

No part of this book may be reproduced in a retrieval system, or transmitted in any form or by any means, electronic, mechanical, photocopying, recording, or otherwise, without the prior written permission of the publisher.

Scripture quotations in this book are taken from the New International Version (NIV), copyright © 1973, 1978, 1984, 2011 by Biblica, Inc.™ All rights reserved worldwide.

This is a work of nonfiction, and the stories within reflect the authors' personal experiences. Some names, identifying details, and events have been altered to protect the privacy of individuals. Any resemblance to actual persons, living or dead, beyond those specified, is purely coincidental.

For those we love,
those we've lost,
&
those who need to hear this...
You are never alone.

CONTENTS

A Note from Trisha   1
A Note from Toni   5
How to Read This Book   9

CHAPTER 1: Cradled in Prayer   13
CHAPTER 2: A Stranger in the Night   21
CHAPTER 3: In His Hands   29
CHAPTER 4: Meeting the Holy Spirit — Take One   37
CHAPTER 5: When Faith Takes Root   43
CHAPTER 6: Meeting the Holy Spirit — Take Two   51
CHAPTER 7: My Little Angel   59
CHAPTER 8: My Perfect Life List   67
CHAPTER 9: A Christmas Miracle   75
CHAPTER 10: The Companion on the Camino   89
CHAPTER 11: Sweet Lord Divine   97

Closing Reflections from Trisha   105
Closing Reflections from Toni   109
Acknowledgements   113
About the Authors   117

A Note from Trisha

My family is probably a lot like yours. We're simple people; nothing about our lives is extravagant. But one thing has always set us apart: our faith. It wasn't always that way for me, though. My spiritual journey wandered from devout Catholic to lost soul, from lapsed Catholic to a proud, "Oh, just try to stop me from being Catholic" Catholic. But even in my struggles, I always felt God beside me.

I credit my mom, Toni, for instilling an unwavering sense of God's presence in me. From an early age, she taught me that I could achieve anything and that God loved me unconditionally. For my first communion, I received a plaque inscribed with the words of Jeremiah 29:11: *"For I know the plans I have for you,"* declares the Lord, *"plans to prosper you and not to harm you, plans to give you hope and a future."* I made a habit of reading it every day, and those words stayed with me, giving me strength and hope whenever life got difficult.

But as much as my faith anchored me growing up, nothing could have prepared me for how life would test it. In my late teens, a traumatic event shattered my sense of self and led me away from God. I spent years feeling lost, spiraling deeper into pain and searching for anything to ease it—even turning to drugs at one point. Even in my lowest moments, the Holy Spirit reached into the dark emotional pits I had fallen into and pulled me out. These encounters were nothing short of divine grace, but

A NOTE FROM TRISHA

I wasn't ready to fully open my heart to God. By my late twenties, I had managed to rebuild my life. I'd found stability after what felt like a lost decade, and landing my dream job at MTV in New York gave me the sense that I was finally on the right path. For a while, I told myself this was enough.

But everything shifted when my dad was diagnosed with terminal heart failure. That Christmas, my family witnessed what we can only describe as a miracle—my dad's recovery. My mom shares the full story in the chapter *A Christmas Miracle,* capturing the incredible details of that event. It was a turning point for me, though not in the way I might have expected. I didn't realize it at the time, but a gnawing thought quietly took hold of me. Unconsciously, I became consumed by the idea that my dad's life could be taken at any moment, and without knowing it, I let that fear shape my choices.

Instead of trusting in God's plan, I fixated on the milestones I thought I needed to reach—not just for myself, but because I wanted my dad to see it all. *I should be more successful. I should be married by now. I should have children.* But when I faced multiple miscarriages, I was devastated. I was convinced that I'd done everything "right," so why did it feel like God was punishing me—or, at the very least, abandoning me?

In my grief, I started to spiral. Cracks in my marriage widened, and as my relationship with my husband crumbled, so did my career. By 2018, I'd lost everything. On a whim, I left for Spain, unable to sit alone with my pain in New York, imagining myself as Julia Roberts in *Eat, Pray, Love.* But a few years later, I was forced to admit that a change of scenery couldn't fix me. I needed to work on myself.

Around then, I discovered the Camino de Santiago—a pilgrimage to the Cathedral of Saint James in Galicia, Spain. The idea of hiking hundreds of miles didn't appeal to me initially, but something inside urged me to go. I convinced myself that time alone in nature would help me sort out my life. Ever since I'd left New York, my mind had been full of heavy questions, all boiling down to this: *If I wasn't a mother, a wife, or a successful executive, then who was I?*

So, I laced up my boots and set out, determined to find answers. But instead of the clarity I expected, I began to understand the true meaning of surrender—of letting go of control and trusting God's plan. That lesson of surrender, along with others about faith, gratitude, and timing, is the heart of the stories in this book.

I've learned that even our brokenness needs to be examined and appreciated. Some of these stories are hard to tell, but I share them because I've seen how God works through our struggles, using them to reveal His love. Now, I feel called to share these experiences with you.

And I think I understand why.

This year marks the 20th anniversary of that extraordinary Christmas miracle in South Texas. For two decades, I've wrestled with its magnitude, unpacking its lessons piece by piece. Now, all I can hear is God's voice urgently telling me, "What are you waiting for? Get out and tell everybody."

That's why my mom and I wrote *Bending Palms*—to proclaim loudly that God is always with us. I'll admit, I hesitated to add *My Perfect Life List* at first, unsure if it truly belonged among these stories. But the more I reflected, the more I saw how it fit. And with that addition, we reached eleven chapters—a number I later learned carries spiritual significance as a reminder of divine guidance and insight. It was as if God Himself was telling me, "Trust the story; it's all part of the plan."

In each chapter, you'll see how God's presence was guiding us—even when we couldn't see it. And that same presence is with you, too, right now, in every moment of your life. He's inviting you to feel His love, to trust His guidance, and to open yourself to the quiet miracles waiting for you. We

A NOTE FROM TRISHA

hope through these stories, you'll find the inspiration to recognize His hand in your journey and the strength to trust in His perfect plan.

May you be inspired and blessed always,
Trisha

A Note from Toni

I've always prayed whenever I've desperately needed something. I think it's because of my Abuelita. Some of my fondest memories are watching her pray the rosary every morning and every night. She would stand by the kitchen window, apron on, with her rosary in one hand and holy water in the other. She kept a little altar in her bedroom with icons and statues on a shelf above her bed. I loved that altar. Even when playing in other parts of the house, I felt safe just knowing it was there. Whenever I see her favorite image of Our Lady of Guadalupe, I still feel that same sense of security.

When I visited Abuelita, I had no choice but to go to Mass with her. We'd get up early on Sunday mornings and walk to church, whether I liked it or not. I obeyed out of fear, but that emotion was the result of my juvenile understanding of God. As I grew in knowledge and faith, I grew in my love for my Lord. I give Abuelita credit for the faith she instilled in me at a young age.

As I grow older, I realize the years seem to pass faster and faster. My mornings are quiet, starting with coffee and time with Jesus. Each day, I thank Him for another day, for all the blessings He has given, for the joyful memories I've shared with family and friends, and even for the heartbreak and tears. Each experience has shaped me into who I am today: a woman who knows she can do all things through Christ, who

A NOTE FROM TONI

strengthens her. So, let me take you on a brief journey of my life—a glimpse into moments I endured and had to overcome.

My name is Antonia Fernandez, but everyone calls me Toni. I was born and raised on the west side of San Antonio, Texas—not Alamo Ranch, but the true *West Side*. As a child, I was blissfully unaware of the struggles my parents faced. Life felt simple—my siblings and I were always having fun playing Jacks, exploring outside, or listening to music and dancing. My dad doted on me, and I was happy.

But before I turned six, everything changed. My parents divorced, and my dad remarried just weeks later. Suddenly, we were distant memories to him; his new family took priority. My mother became a single parent to ten children without help or resources. She didn't speak English, had little education, and had no work experience. Back then, there was no such thing as child support, welfare, or food stamps. We survived on government cheese, powdered eggs, canned peanut butter, and a "mystery" meat that, to this day, I still can't identify. My mother was gone most of the day, looking for work, and we were left alone... vulnerable.

One family member took advantage of her absence, and at the age of eight, I became a victim of sexual assault. During that dark time, I hid in a closet and prayed—yes, prayed—to Jesus, asking Him to protect me and keep me hidden. I couldn't tell anyone and being so young, I believed the threats he made against my family if I spoke up. Today, I'm proud to say I've dealt with the trauma of that experience, but getting to a place of forgiveness took a miracle—one I describe in the chapter *My Little Angel*.

As a teenager in the 1970s, I was a good girl—mostly because I was terrified of my mom! I worked odd jobs to help pay for family essentials and eventually landed a job at a department store. That's where I met David, a cute stock boy with chunky Buddy Holly glasses—not exactly my type at first. But he was sweet and persistent, and after a kite-flying date, I fell for him. Hard. Looking back, I see it was all part of God's plan.

Together, David and I built a beautiful life. We raised two daughters, Trisha and Lisa, and surrounded ourselves with friends and family who bless our lives every day. Through it all, my faith has been the steady thread that's held me together, especially during my most challenging moments.

Life has shown me that we'll all be tested no matter how faithful we are. But with each struggle, our resilience grows. That's why I'm so proud to share this book. When Trisha asked if I'd tell some of my stories, I knew my prayers had been answered. I've watched my daughter's relationship with God evolve through her struggles, and I always prayed for Him to care for her. Reading her part of this book, I was overwhelmed by just how present God has been.

Faith isn't hard to find—it's surrendering to God's plan that's difficult, especially when it doesn't match our own. In the stories I share, like *Cradled in Prayer* and *In His Hands*, I hope to remind you, as I was reminded, that no matter what you're facing, God is always there, waiting to walk beside you.

God Bless,
Toni

How to Read This Book

Bending Palms was born from a deep love for God, a desire to share moments of divine intervention, and countless cups of coffee. Join us on a journey through big and small moments, guided by grace and strengthened by faith. Here are a few friendly suggestions for getting the most out of these pages:

1. Come as You Are
We wrote this book for real life, not perfect lives. Bring your whole self—doubts, hopes, fears, and all. Our stories may have some messy bits, and we're pretty sure yours do, too. You're in good company here.

2. Take a Closer Look
Though each story in *Bending Palms* is deeply personal, it was written for *you*. If you look closely, you may find your story reflected within ours. If so, honor that. We are children in Christ, and many of the themes and lessons explored in this book are universal. We hope by sharing our story, we may help some of you embrace yours.

3. Pause and Ponder
At the end of each chapter, you'll find questions that invite you to pause, reflect, or even scribble down a few thoughts if you're a note-taker (or a doodler—we don't judge). You could even discuss the

questions with a friend or family member—preferably one who doesn't mind a little deep conversation over a cup of joe.

4. Spend Time with the Scriptures
Each chapter opens with a passage from Scripture to frame the story. Take a moment with these verses—they can offer wisdom, strength, or a gentle nudge from above. Think of them as little messages to carry with you as you read.

And now that we got some business out of the way... welcome to *Bending Palms*. We hope these stories bless you as much as sharing them has blessed us.

When you pass through the waters, I will be with you; and when you pass through the rivers, they will not sweep over you. When you walk through the fire, you will not be burned; the flames will not set you ablaze. For I am the Lord your God, the Holy One of Israel, your Savior.

—ISAIAH 43:2-3

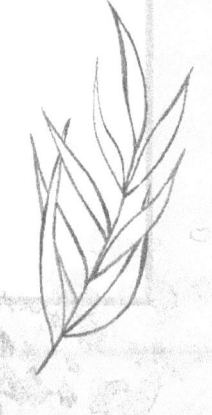

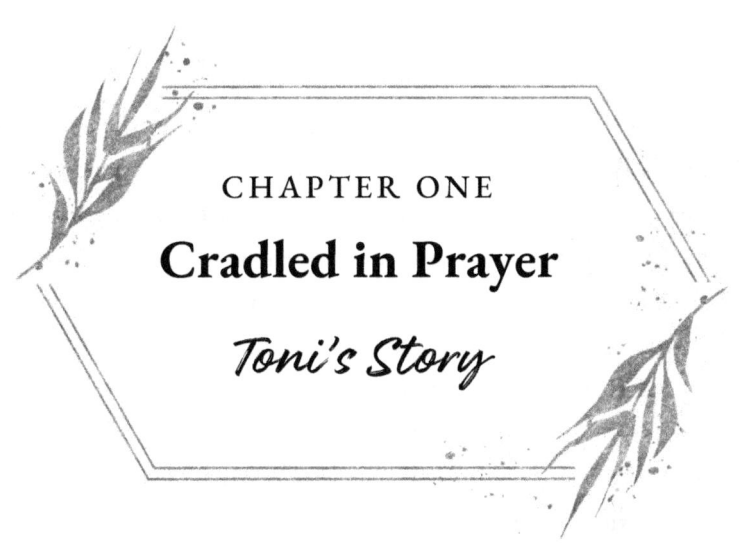

CHAPTER ONE
Cradled in Prayer
Toni's Story

I was only twenty when I faced the most terrifying moment of my life. My pregnancy with Trisha started perfectly. I was young and healthy, and David and I were excited to start our family. By all accounts, I should have been overjoyed. Yet, despite all these blessings, I was struggling with my faith. I felt distant from God, burdened by unresolved pain from my childhood that I couldn't seem to let go of.

So when I found out I was pregnant, I didn't turn to God right away. I told myself it was enough to celebrate with David and focus on the joy of starting a family. But the truth was harder to face: I couldn't thank God for this blessing because a part of me didn't want to. It felt like giving Him credit for something good would invalidate all the hurt I was still carrying. Ignoring Him was easier than confronting the weight of my anger. But when my body began to betray me, I found myself questioning everything.

"Toni, we're going to need to put you on complete bed rest and a restricted diet. Just as a precaution," my doctor said, his tone tinged with concern.

As I nodded, a thought crept in: *What am I going to do if there's something wrong with my baby?* Then another followed: *Why haven't I been talking to God?* The questions unsettled me, but I pushed them aside. I just needed to follow instructions and trust everything would be fine.

But as the weeks stretched on, despite following the doctor's orders, my symptoms persisted. I was constantly exhausted, and my blood pressure was creeping higher. The appointments became more frequent, and by the eighth month, I could tell something had shifted.

"Toni, we need to admit you to the hospital," my doctor said sternly. "You're running a fever. The baby isn't growing as expected, and we need to do more tests." His words sent a wave of panic through me.

"What does that mean?" I asked, barely recognizing my own voice.

"It means we're going to do everything we can to figure out why your baby isn't developing as she should," he replied, his gaze compassionate but unwavering.

The thought of something being wrong with my baby was unbearable, and I wanted to lean on my husband. But David's family was moving back to El Paso that weekend, and I didn't want him to worry. "I'll be fine," I assured him as he dropped me off the next morning. "It's just a few tests, and I'll be in good hands." But as soon as I was alone, I regretted not telling him how terrified I truly was.

The nurses got to work once I was settled in my hospital room. They drew blood, collected a urine sample, and fired off what felt like a hundred questions. Then came the sonogram. The probe glided across my belly as the steady hum of the machine filled the quiet room. I glanced at the nurse. Her brow creased for a split second before she smoothed her expression and turned back to the screen. My stomach tightened.

After that, there was nothing to do but wait. I sat alone, listening to the faint sounds of the hospital around me. Every time I heard footsteps in the hallway, my heart jumped. I kept hoping for good news but braced myself for the worst. After what felt like forever, my doctor finally came in, his face tense.

"Is David here?" he asked.

I shook my head, my heart pounding. "He's with his family... he'll be here soon," I said, hoping that was true.

The doctor took a deep breath, his voice carefully measured as he spoke. "Toni, the baby's in trouble. Your bloodwork shows signs of toxemia, and we're concerned that the amniotic fluid may be putting your baby's life at serious risk. We'll need to do an amniocentesis. If the results confirm our suspicions, we may need to perform an emergency C-section."

"No," I whispered, clutching the sides of the hospital bed. "You're going to cut me open?" The thought was overwhelming.

After a few more minutes of conversation, he left, and a deep sense of dread settled over me. Pressing my palms together in a desperate plea, I started to pray, "God, please. Don't let anything happen to my baby. I know I haven't talked to You in a long time. But I need You. I *need* You now."

The words tumbled out in broken sobs, and I worried my cries wouldn't make it to Heaven. Or if they did, maybe God wouldn't answer them. *Why had I walked away from Him?*

My body suddenly felt like it was shutting down. A deep fatigue weakened my muscles, and I started to sweat profusely. Seconds later, I felt vomit burn the back of my throat before erupting onto the floor beside me. Nurses rushed in with cool towels, pressing them to my forehead, doing their best to calm me. "Just breathe, Toni," one murmured, but her worried eyes scared me even more.

Then, a rush of warmth quickly spread over me. "I think my water broke," I said breathlessly. The nurse lifted the pad that was beneath me and went pale. The amniotic fluid that was on it was a dark, pea-colored green. *My baby's swimming in that?* I began to vomit more forcefully.

"Call her doctor. *Now*," the nurse screamed.

Moments later, my doctor appeared, his face tight with urgency. "We need to deliver your baby—immediately." I braced myself for the idea that my baby would need to be cut from my womb. But as he examined me, his expression softened. "Toni, forget the C-section. We're going to try for a natural delivery."

Though my body felt like it was being crushed from the inside out, I felt a twinge of relief—soon, my baby would be safe. But the delivery dragged on, each moment feeling like an eternity.

When Trisha finally arrived, the room was eerily quiet. I didn't hear her cry. Instead, someone urgently yelled, "She's not breathing!" My eyes darted around the room, searching frantically, but I only caught a glimpse of my daughter's tiny face before they whisked her away. Weighing only four pounds and struggling for air, she was rushed to a nearby hospital with a neonatal unit better equipped to care for her.

In recovery, I waited alone, my chest tight and knotted with tension. A while later, David arrived, his face pale and his eyes wet with tears. He took my hand, his voice trembling as he said, "She's okay for now." I let out a deep sigh of relief.

"But the doctor told me he almost lost both of you."

I didn't believe what I'd heard. As a first-time mother, I'd assumed all that pain and sickness was just part of childbirth. But seeing David's face and hearing his words, the gravity of all that happened finally sank in. At that moment, a shiver ran through me—not from fear, but from realizing how fragile life really is.

I could have died. Trisha could have died. The life David and I had imagined together, raising her, watching her grow, could have disappeared before it began. And yet, here I was—alive—and my baby daughter was fighting for her life. I hadn't fully understood, until that moment, how close we had come to losing everything.

Once David was sure I'd be okay, he squeezed my hand and rushed to check on our daughter.

The following day, a pediatric doctor visited me. "The next seventy-two hours are critical. She's still struggling," he said, his voice grave. "And due to the lack of oxygen in the womb, if she does make it, there's a strong chance that she may be slower mentally and physically than other children."

I resolved then and there to love her fiercely, no matter what challenges lay ahead. "Doctor, I don't care about any of that," I said. "I just want her to have a chance. I just want her to live."

The day they discharged me, I didn't wait for the nurses to bring a wheelchair; I ran out, desperate to get to the NICU to see my baby.

On the drive to the children's hospital, David gently warned me about what I would see. "She has needles in her hands, feet, even her head," he said, his voice thick with emotion. It broke my heart to picture her like that, but I knew she was a fighter—like her mother... like her grandmother.

We put on gowns, masks, and shoe covers when we arrived. Following the nurse, my heart pounded as we approached a large machine connected to a tiny, frail infant, its steady rhythm filling the room. My knees felt weak. *Is that my baby?*

"Please, God," I prayed softly. "Don't let that be her."

The nurse led us past the machine. *Thank You, Jesus.* Just a few steps later, there she was—my Trisha, lying peacefully in an incubator, no needles attached. The tubes had been removed that morning. She looked like a delicate little doll.

My heart overflowed with love and relief when they finally let me hold her. As I cradled her, I felt the weight of all we'd been through together. When David held her next, I saw his hand tremble and his forehead glisten, as the nurse wiped away his sweat. She was so fragile in our arms, yet strong in ways we couldn't yet fully understand.

Trisha spent nine days in neonatal care, her body gaining strength daily. In those quiet moments beside her incubator, I realized I had been the one keeping God at a distance, holding on to my pain instead of trusting Him with it. But through this trial, it became clear: He had been with us all along, holding Trisha and me. Overwhelmed with gratitude, I thanked Him for this blessing, whispering, "I don't deserve this, but thank You." I promised to lean on Him and trust in His strength from that moment forward. I knew I'd need His guidance for whatever lay ahead, but for the first time in a long time, I felt at peace.

When Trisha had grown strong enough to be discharged, we brought her home. During those first few months, we hovered over her, monitoring every movement and breath. Though the doctors had warned us of possible developmental challenges, I knew she would defy every expectation and blossom into a healthy, vibrant child who excelled at everything she tried.

A few years later, when I missed a period, unease swept over me, and memories of that first pregnancy flooded back. But now, my faith was different. I surrendered my fears, whispering, "Let it be Your will, Lord." When my doctor confirmed my second pregnancy, I entrusted everything to God, praying every step of the way. Nine months later, I had Lisa, a perfectly healthy seven-pound angel.

God had shown me His mercy, holding me close in life's darkest hours. With every breath, I felt His love, His unwavering faithfulness. And from that moment forward, I was determined never to walk alone again.

REFLECTIONS

Recall a time when you faced a situation that felt overwhelming or beyond your control. How did you see—or seek—God's hand in those moments?

How does faith in God's presence change how you navigate fear or uncertainty? What might it look like to invite God into your heart during moments of anxiety or doubt?

What does it mean to trust in God's protection for those you love? How can you deepen that trust, especially when you feel helpless or afraid?

Do not forget to show hospitality to strangers, for by so doing some people have shown hospitality to angels without knowing it.

—HEBREWS 13:2

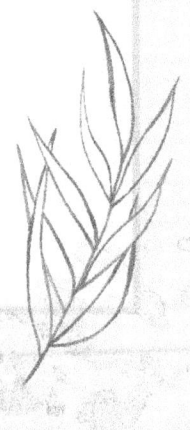

CHAPTER TWO
A Stranger in the Night
Trisha's Story

I've been listening to the story of my birth for as long as I can remember. Mom and Dad loved telling it, and frankly, I really enjoyed hearing it. But it wasn't until a few years ago that my parents told me another story—about how my dad was a sick baby and a strange man had appeared in the middle of the night, seemingly out of nowhere, to save his life. At first, I thought, *Oh, come on. That's too strange to be true.* But after speaking to my grandpa and doing some of my own research, I had to admit—it was a perfect little example of the magic of faith.

The story begins in late 1954 in El Paso, Texas. My grandparents, David and Ana, were newlyweds—young Mexican immigrants who had just moved to the United States, hoping to build a better life for their growing family. Neither of them spoke English, and they struggled to make ends meet. They lived in a small, two-room wooden "house" just off Madera Avenue, a street that had yet to be paved. Their bathroom was a simple outhouse. To stay warm, Ana used a tin tub she'd found as a makeshift fireplace, filling it with hot charcoal before bath time.

It was winter, and their newborn son—my dad, David Jr.—was sick. The little house provided hardly any warmth; the wooden walls had gaps and holes, and my grandpa had lined them with cardboard to keep the chill out. But on the coldest nights, cardboard wasn't enough.

One evening, Ana grew anxious as her baby's condition worsened, his cries echoing through the drafty rooms. She held him close, whispering prayers, begging for God to intervene. But as the hours dragged on and his condition didn't improve, her distress turned into desperation.

"Haz algo," she said, begging her husband to do something about their son's suffering.

But as my grandpa later explained, "Mija, I didn't know what to do. We didn't own a phone. We used one at a store sometimes, but it was far. And it was night—not too dark yet, but storming. There was so much water and mud, and I didn't have a car. We didn't know what to do."

But Ana wouldn't stop pleading with David to find a way to help their son. She was as desperate and inconsolable as her wailing baby. She needed something more substantial than prayers, but what? What could they do?

As they sat helplessly, a sudden bang at the front door startled them. They jumped to their feet, their eyes meeting in alarm. Who could it be? They only knew one other person in El Paso—a neighbor they rarely spoke to.

"It would've been strange if it were him," my grandpa explained to me.

Ana and David stood frozen, spooked by the sound amid the storm's chaos. Then came another bang. Ana's mind raced. Who would be out there in such terrible weather? A thought struck her: maybe whoever it was could help. Maybe they had a car or could get their baby to a hospital.

"Ábrela," Ana snapped, urging her husband to see who was outside.

David hesitated, then opened the door slowly. What he saw shocked him. A slender black man stood in the rain, drenched from head to toe.

"He had on a long black coat and a black hat," Grandpa told me. "With so much rain pouring down, it was hard to see the man's face at first. I thought I was imaging things. It was strange to see someone all dressed in black at my front door in the middle of a storm. It scared me."

But when David looked closer, the man's calm expression and the kindness in his eyes eased some of his fear.

"¿Es aquí donde hay un niño enfermo?" the man asked calmly, his Spanish perfect.

Stunned, David didn't immediately respond. How could the stranger have known there was a sick child there? Then David noticed the doctor's bag clutched in the man's hand.

"Sí, sí, pero..." David stammered, at a loss for words.

Peering over her husband's shoulder, Ana saw the man and immediately understood—her prayers were being answered. Help had arrived.

But David was still reluctant. The shock of the stranger's sudden appearance in the violent storm made him wary. Ana's voice, however, broke through his doubt.

"Déjalo pasar. Déjalo pasar *ahora*," she insisted.

With their son's anguished cries growing louder, David quickly stepped aside and ushered the man into their home.

"He just walked inside, like it was all very normal, Mija," Grandpa explained. "And he went straight to your daddy. I don't remember exactly what happened next. I don't remember if he did something or gave him medicine. But I do know that just a few moments later, he told us, 'Your son is going to be okay.' And then he just smiled and left. He didn't ask for money. He didn't say how he knew that your daddy needed help. He just walked out the door and into the rain again. Soon after that, your daddy stopped crying."

Later, as I thought about my grandpa's story, I realized I had a lot more questions. Why hadn't I heard about this before? All these years, my parents had been telling everyone the story of how I was born sick and then got better. Why hadn't I heard about my dad's remarkable healing when he was a baby?

"Well, I heard the story when I was young, and I told your mom about it," my dad explained. "But it wasn't until she and I were watching a movie just a few years ago that something jogged that memory again. It was a film about Saint Martin de Porres. He was a priest from Lima in the 1600s who had studied medicine. In the movie, they showed him appearing in random places as a doctor. In one scene, he suddenly appears on a battlefield, helps the wounded, and then disappears again." As my dad spoke, his words poured out faster and faster. I could tell he was excited to be retelling the story. "And he especially helped sick children. Your mom and I just looked at each other, taken aback by the similarity to the story of the stranger who visited me when I was a baby."

Incredulous, I continued to push. "But... you don't know what he looked like. It could've been anybody that night. Why were you convinced it was Saint Martin?"

"Well, that's why we asked Grandma and Grandpa to watch the movie," Dad told me. "And you should've seen them. They were both shouting, 'That was him. That was him.'"

I decided to investigate, and what my dad said was true. Saint Martin de Porres was known for his miracles, especially among the poor and sick, and was often said to appear in times of need. Still, I wanted to hear it directly from Grandpa.

"Grandpa, I've grown up hearing a lot of stories about saints and miracles, but I never heard you talk about this before."

"Yes, Mija, it's true," he explained. "I don't know why I didn't talk about it before. I think that changed when I started going to church more regularly and went on a retreat. That's when I told people the story, and they believed me. They said it was true—that miracles happen. I know my memory is fading now, but I will never forget what happened that night. It happened just like I told you."

"And Grandma? When did she realize that Saint Martin showed up to help Dad?" I asked.

"Oh, after your grandma saw that movie, she knew it was him. She even started collecting little *santitos* of him and asking him to pray for her. It was a beautiful thing." Grandpa wiped a tear from his cheek before he added, "She believed, Mija. There was no other explanation. For years, we tried to understand it. But today we have no doubt that Saint Martin is who God sent to heal my son that night. It happened, and we believe."

Seeing the tenderness in my grandpa's eyes, I couldn't deny what happened that night either. So, I chose to believe in the incredible story, too. Saint Martin de Porres did arrive that stormy night to help two young, desperate parents and their newborn son. And why not?

This story reminds us that miracles can find us even in the darkest places and simplest moments, especially when we're at the edge of our strength. They may not always come in grand, obvious ways, but they reveal themselves in the quiet acts of grace that change our lives forever. For my family, that night was one such miracle—a moment when faith became real when an answered prayer arrived dressed in a long black coat.

REFLECTIONS

Reflect on a time when you felt a sense of divine intervention, perhaps through an unexpected person or moment. How did it shape your understanding of God's care for you?

How open are you to seeing God's presence in everyday encounters or in strangers? What might change if you believed that each interaction is an opportunity for God to reach you or work through you?

Think of a time when someone unexpectedly extended help or compassion to you, especially when you felt alone or in need. How might you be that source of support or comfort for others? Who in your life might need an encouraging word or a listening ear that you can offer today?

*If I say, "Surely the darkness will hide me
and the light become night around me,"
even the darkness will not be dark to you;
the night will shine like the day, for
darkness is as light to you.*

—PSALM 139:11-12

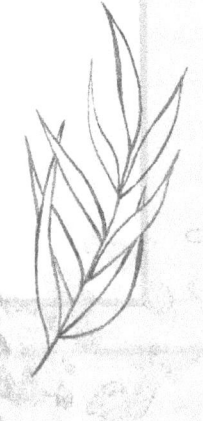

CHAPTER THREE
In His Hands
Toni's Story

In my introduction, I shared a chapter of my life that remains raw to this day, a piece of the past I tried to keep buried. But as hard as it is to look back, it's a moment that shaped my journey with God and deserves to be shared. Dealing with such extreme trauma helped me understand His place in my life.

As a child, I carried a secret too heavy to share. That secret, along with the scars from my parent's divorce, followed me well into adulthood—even through my teenage years and early marriage when I pretended I was fine, convincing myself I could hold it all together. But underneath the facade, I was falling apart. Panic attacks and depression haunted me, and I hid my tears whenever I could—under the cover of a hot shower, behind closed doors, or in stolen moments alone. Most days, it felt like I was stumbling through complete darkness.

David and I had been married a few years when he got transferred to Houston. At first, the change was exciting—a new city, our little apartment, and the promise of fresh experiences. Having spent my whole life in San Antonio, I saw it as an adventure. We played tourist, explored the city, and made happy memories in our cozy little space. But the novelty wore off sooner than I expected. David's job kept him away for long hours, and I was left alone with Trisha, who was still young and a handful. I loved being a mother, but the nights were lonely, and I deeply missed San Antonio and the family I left behind. Long-distance calls were a luxury back then, so our conversations were brief. Instead of helping, the quick calls made me feel even more disconnected; so much was left unsaid.

One day at the playground, I met a woman who lived across the street from us. She had two daughters close to Trisha's age, and they became fast friends. For me, the woman was a lifeline. She distracted me from my pain and helped keep the loneliness away. Before long, though, our friendship revolved around one thing—spending afternoons by the pool with a drink in hand. It started innocently enough with casual cocktails to pass the time, but it quickly became an everyday habit. Her sister, who often joined us but never drank, would sit nearby to keep an eye on the kids.

I turned to alcohol to escape. It dulled the memories I was desperate to forget, but only for a little while. The relief never lasted, and the hangovers brought their own kind of misery. This behavior went on for over a year, each glass of wine or cocktail numbing the pain but never taking it away.

One evening by the pool, we sat watching the sunset through the haze of alcohol when a thought struck me that I couldn't ignore. *I was becoming my mother.*

My mom, who had raised ten children on her own, was the strongest person I knew—my rock and my hero. Yet, I had also watched her struggle with drinking, using it to dull her own sorrows and loneliness. She had sacrificed everything for us, carrying a pain I had never fully understood until that moment. I loved her dearly, but seeing her dependence on alcohol had left a mark. The realization shook me—I didn't want this for myself, for my daughter, or for my marriage.

I began to feel a persistent tugging in my heart—a pull that grew stronger each day. I couldn't shake the feeling that there was more to life and that I was missing something. It was then that I thought of my neighbor's sister. She would often talk about God while we lounged by the pool. Though I usually brushed her off, I now felt an inexplicable urge to reach out. I dialed her number and asked if I could join her prayer group.

She welcomed me with open arms.

As I walked into that room full of women, singing and lifting their hands in praise, I felt like an outsider, unsure if I belonged. I sat awkwardly, feeling out of place, and wondered what I had gotten myself into. The music was strange—nothing like the solemn, reverent songs I was used to at my former church. And the women seemed so free... so joyful. I was nervous, almost certain that I'd made a mistake in coming.

When the speaker took the podium, she began with an inviting, gentle smile. But as she read Scripture, sharing a message of love and redemption, my mind kept wandering. I felt nervous and uneasy. Soon, my thoughts spun out of control, screaming at me to escape. *This is a cult. I need to get out of here.* But then, the woman paused, and I felt her eyes settle on me. She asked the woman behind me to place her hands on my shoulders, and I froze, my muscles tensing in resistance. I was ready to bolt.

Then she spoke directly to me, her voice steady and filled with compassion. "My child," she began, her tone gentle and full of reassurance, "I love you. I have never left you. I have always been by your side."

It felt like the words weren't coming from her but from somewhere far greater. A wave of unexpected comfort washed over me. The tension in my shoulders eased, and though the message wasn't specific, it felt deeply personal, as though it was meant just for me. I sat still, caught off guard by the sudden sense of peace.

Then she continued, recounting moments from my childhood with impossible accuracy. "Do you remember when you would hide in the closet, praying that he wouldn't find you? I was there, by your side, holding you, wiping away your sorrows."

I blinked, stunned and overwhelmed. How could she know the struggles I had kept hidden? Tears began to stream down my face.

Then she spoke of another memory I hadn't shared with a soul. "And those nights when you watched out the window, praying that the bus would bring your mother home safely—I stood beside you, holding your small, clasped hands." I continued to sob, her words uncovering places I had buried for so long.

At the end of her message, there was a call to prayer. I walked forward, as if in a trance, and allowed the women to gather around me. As they prayed, heat radiated from my feet and climbed to my face, igniting something I had never felt before. Without warning, unfamiliar words poured out of my mouth. I couldn't stop them, and soon, I was speaking in a language I didn't recognize. Another woman nearby translated the words I didn't understand. I was terrified and awestruck, caught up in something I couldn't comprehend.

Afterward, they explained that I had received the "gift of tongues" and that the other woman had been given the gift of interpretation. It was an experience beyond words, a moment when I felt the undeniable presence of God. I knew then He had been with me through every dark moment and silent prayer I had ever whispered.

I left that prayer group transformed. The weight I had carried was gone, replaced by an unfamiliar lightness. The urge to drink vanished, replaced by a hunger to draw closer to God and to feel His love and guidance in every part of my life.

I started working at a local preschool, taking Trisha with me each day. It was the perfect escape from the routine that had trapped me, giving me purpose and a new direction.

God had shown me His grace, lifting me from a darkness I thought I'd never escape. And from that moment on, I knew that no matter what, I was held firmly, lovingly, in His hands.

REFLECTIONS

Reflect on a time when you carried a burden alone or hid a painful part of yourself. How did that experience shape you, and what could it look like to invite God into those hidden places?

This chapter describes being lifted from darkness into a place of healing and peace. When have you experienced a "turning point" in your life, a moment that brought unexpected hope or clarity? How might God have been present for you, even if you couldn't see it then?

Sometimes, stepping out of isolation and opening ourselves to others can be profoundly transformative. Who are the people or communities that help you feel seen and supported? What role might faith and connection play in your own healing journey?

But the Advocate, the Holy Spirit, whom the Father will send in my name, will teach you all things and will remind you of everything I have said to you. Peace I leave with you; my peace I give you. I do not give to you as the world gives. Do not let your hearts be troubled and do not be afraid.

—JOHN 14:26-27

CHAPTER FOUR

Meeting the Holy Spirit — Take One

Trisha's Story

I was raised in the Catholic Church—literally. After school, Mom would take me to her office at Holy Spirit Parish where I'd do my homework or help her file some paperwork. Even my first job was working for the church, though I didn't do much more than make copies and play with the younger kids in the afterschool program who were waiting for their parents to pick them up.

Since I spent so much time at church, I was used to hearing some pretty strange stories. Once, in a hushed whisper, I heard Mom mention to her co-worker that a family needed Father to bless their house because of all the "activity" happening there. Then there was the time a woman came into the office, begging Father to step outside and talk to her son, who was sitting in the car. She explained that he had changed into someone she didn't recognize—and she was afraid for her life.

Sometimes, the strangeness followed us. Mom and I once shared a room when we slept over at a cousin's house. In the middle of the night, Mom shot up so forcefully that she woke me. Before my eyes could even adjust to the darkness, I heard her speaking in strange gibberish. Frightened, I tried to shake her, but she wouldn't budge. Then, less than a minute later, she threw herself back onto the pillow and was out again. The following day, when I told her that she scared the *bejeezus* out of me, she told me she had a very vivid dream that she was talking to Jesus. That was when I learned that my mom spoke in tongues.

I started going on teen retreats a couple of times a year. It didn't feel like I was making a grand spiritual gesture. Those weekends away with my friends felt like an extension of my everyday life. I didn't see attending them as me trying to get closer to God. It was just nice to get away from my parents' watchful eyes.

But as I got older and started dating, I realized I didn't want to spend my time at some dank retreat house. There were more exciting ways to spend a Saturday night. I started to resent the handful of times each year when I'd be asked to go on retreat as a participant or team leader. But in my senior year of high school, something happened that changed me forever.

Knowing I was soon going off to college, I signed up for one last retreat. They needed volunteers, and I had been feeling guilty for letting the staff and my retreat friends down. So, I committed to being there. But a few weeks before the retreat, I found myself in a very dangerous situation.

It was a weekend like any other. I was staying at a friend's house, and we decided to do something stupid. We snuck out of the house and went with another friend to her boyfriend's house. We listened to music and drank beer, planning to be gone only an hour or two.

But when plans changed, and I found myself drunk and alone with my friend's boyfriend, the unthinkable happened. He forced himself on me, and I was powerless to stop him. Afterward, confused and burdened with unbearable shame, I acted as if I had been a willing participant. I wasn't—but I didn't know what to call it at the time. So, I pretended I was in control. A victim? No, that wasn't me. I wouldn't let that version be my story.

And so, carrying this secret, I showed up to the retreat, mocking myself for claiming to be a leader when I felt weak and broken. I hated the fact that I was there. Throughout the weekend, I watched the younger, carefree participants and envied them. All I wanted to do was get out of there.

When we gathered for our final activity of the weekend, we were asked to sit silently, with our eyes closed, and reflect on the experience, praying for guidance and understanding. I did no such thing. Instead, sitting on the bench with my eyes shut and head hung low, I replayed that night over and over. Through soft music, I heard others crying as usually happened, and I felt disdain for their tenderness. *Be strong,* I told myself. The thought ran through my head, and I chased it, trying to trap it, tame it, and embody it.

Suddenly, a strong, warm hand found my shoulder. The darkness turned bright orange, and I fell forward onto my knees. Waves of tears fell from my clenched eyes as the warmth that started on my shoulder spread throughout my body. The sensation was not unlike a hug—only it was one hundred times more soothing. Its gentle power pushed away the tension I'd been carrying. For a few moments, I felt a release from my pain and could see a future where I would no longer be defined by my experience that night.

And while I could've felt guilty for reluctantly attending the retreat, thinking of it only as an obligation, I didn't—because there was no judgment at that moment. Instead, I felt seen and loved, and I felt immensely grateful that I met the Holy Spirit in one of my darkest moments.

I wish I could say that once I left the retreat, I learned how to talk about the pain I felt, so I could learn to manage it. But that wasn't the direction my path would take. I continued to punish myself and suffer for many years. Though my journey wasn't easy, that moment at the retreat sparked something in me—a quiet confirmation that I wasn't alone, no matter how hard things became.

Over the years, when I felt lost or overwhelmed, the memory of that embrace from the Holy Spirit guided me back to my faith more than once. It carried me through the darkest valleys and eventually led me toward the light.

REFLECTIONS

Have you ever felt the presence of the Holy Spirit in a way that brought you peace or clarity, especially when you were struggling? What was that experience like, and how did it impact your faith?

In moments when life feels heavy, how open are you to inviting the Holy Spirit's guidance? What might it look like to surrender your burdens and allow God's Spirit to bring you comfort and direction?

How have challenging or painful experiences shaped your relationship with faith? Have you ever found strength, healing, or clarity in moments when you least expected it?

Then he told them many things in parables, saying: "A farmer went out to sow his seed. As he was scattering the seed, some fell along the path, and the birds came and ate it up. Some fell on rocky places, where it did not have much soil. It sprang up quickly, because the soil was shallow. But when the sun came up, the plants were scorched, and they withered because they had no root. Other seed fell among thorns, which grew up and choked the plants. Still other seed fell on good soil, where it produced a crop—a hundred, sixty, or thirty times what was sown."

—MATTHEW 13:3-9

CHAPTER FIVE
When Faith Takes Root
Toni's Story

During the first five years of my marriage to David, our lives underwent many changes. One of the biggest surprises was moving back to San Antonio. David had been growing weary of his job in Houston, and a co-worker told him about a position at a new company. During the interview, they asked if he'd be open to relocating. We could hardly believe it when he learned the position was in San Antonio. David got the job, and we packed up and moved back home.

We bought our first house—a cozy and beautiful place off Callaghan and Culebra. It was everything I had dreamed of: a sanctuary where our family could thrive. Not long after, Lisa was born. She was a healthy, perfect baby. For the first time in a long time, I felt whole. My heart was brimming with joy and gratitude.

Our new home brought many wonderful changes, especially within my family. My oldest brother, Joe, started visiting more, becoming "Uncle Joe" to my daughters. He bonded with Lisa, stopping by on his days off to spend time with her, creating memories I would always cherish.

The most unexpected blessing came that Christmas when Joe started bringing my father with him. I hadn't spoken to my dad in several years, and I knew he wasn't coming willingly—Joe was nudging him to come along. But I was willing to take what I could get; I wanted to meet my father as an adult, get to know him, and form the kind of relationship with him that my oldest siblings had. With God now at the center of my life, my heart was open. I was ready to forgive him for abandoning us. I cherished each visit, even if brief. Seeing him with my girls, watching him interact with Joe, and reconnecting with him filled me with peace. It felt like life was finally falling into place.

But just as I settled into this new happiness, another change came and yanked me away. David was transferred to Laredo just eight months after we arrived in San Antonio. I was devastated. I'd only just begun rebuilding a relationship with my father, and without Joe acting as the bridge, I worried our fragile connection would vanish. *How could we be leaving already?*

Our house in San Antonio sold on the first day it went on the market. Everything happened so quickly that I didn't have a chance to say goodbye to my dad. I cried the entire drive to Laredo, feeling as though my heart had shattered. When we arrived, I looked at the small, dreary house we'd rented, and my heart sank. The place felt dark and oppressive, filled with a heavy energy that seemed almost hostile. Inside, the walls felt like they were closing in around me, watching me. I was constantly nervous and on edge. It seemed that what I sensed in my surroundings had also started to take root inside me—a feeling of profound wrongness as if something within me was beginning to rot.

Trisha started kindergarten, and David's new job required him to travel frequently, leaving me alone in the unfamiliar place. I was isolated, missing my mom's comforting presence, my brothers and sisters' laughter, and, most of all, the precious moments I'd spent with my dad. I had dreamed of sitting with him, asking him questions about his life, and hearing the stories that had shaped him. I wanted to know what he thought about me, what he had hoped for me as his daughter. But that chance was slipping away.

But my heartache didn't turn into depression—it turned into anger. I was furious with God. "How could You do this to me?" I demanded. "You know how much I longed for a relationship with my father. How could You take it away?"

I stopped praying and reading the Bible. Every thought of God upset me; the pain felt sharper because I had trusted Him so profoundly. I thought about the Scripture from Job 1:21: *"The Lord gave and the Lord has taken away; may the name of the Lord be praised."* But it brought no comfort—only more resentment. I couldn't understand why God had allowed me to feel the beginnings of hope in San Antonio—why He'd let me believe that the wounds from my childhood, the years of abandonment and hurt, might finally start to mend.

Soon, my anger turned to rage, pushing me to a place I didn't recognize. Every mention of God felt like salt in a wound, and I wanted nothing to do with Him. But God, in His grace, had a way of reaching me even in my stubbornness.

One day, I sat in the kitchen with Lisa, peeling a pear and feeding slices to her. For some reason, I felt an urge to cut into the pear's seeds. As I stared at the seeds, something tugged at me—a sense that I needed to know what was inside. The feeling grew stronger, and frustration bubbled up inside me. I looked up at the ceiling and shouted, "What? What are You trying to tell me?"

Even though I had turned away from Him, something pushed me to act. Almost without realizing it, I picked up my Bible—a book I hadn't touched in months—and opened it. My eyes fell on the Parable of the Sower in Matthew, and it was like a light switched on inside me. God had been speaking to me all along, and at that moment, I finally listened.

In the parable, Jesus tells the story of a farmer scattering seeds. Some seeds fall on the path and are eaten by birds; others land on rocky ground, where they sprout quickly but die because they lack deep roots. Still others fall among thorns and are choked, while only the seeds on good soil grow strong and bear fruit.

At that moment, I knew—I was the seed planted on rocky ground. I had received God's word joyfully but hadn't allowed it to take root. When life became difficult, my faith withered away. I'd been so quick to lose sight of His presence as soon as things didn't go my way.

Overcome with this realization, I dropped to my knees, tears streaming down my face. "God, forgive me," I sobbed as the truth of my actions weighed on me. Then, in an instant, a warmth surrounded me—a familiar, loving embrace. It was as if God Himself was wrapping me in His arms, a feeling I'd first experienced at that prayer group. In the quiet, I heard Him speak to my heart: *"My child, I love you. I will never leave you, for I am your Father. I have given you all you needed—everything your earthly father couldn't provide. I have given you My unconditional love."*

A peace I can't fully describe washed over me, and once again, words I didn't understand flowed from my mouth in a language that wasn't my own. Between the tears and prayers, the meaning became clear, as though God was whispering directly to my soul: *"Go in peace, My child. I will be close by when you are heartbroken and comfort you all the days of your life. For I am your Father, and you will forever be My daughter."*

All my anger melted away in that moment, replaced by a deep and humbling gratitude. I had thrown a tantrum and let bitterness fester. But God hadn't turned away. He had been with me all along, patiently waiting for me to see.

Once again, I knew with unshakable certainty that I was never alone, no matter where life took me. And as I knelt there, I found the strength to trust Him again, to believe that He was guiding me—even through the places I didn't want to go. His love was my constant anchor, and I felt ready to move forward, knowing He was with me every step of the way.

REFLECTIONS

How do you respond when life uproots your plans or distances you from loved ones? Consider the reassurance that comes from trusting God's plan, even when it's difficult. This trust can bring a sense of comfort and security, helping you find peace amid life's uncertainties.

The Parable of the Sower speaks of seeds that flourish only when planted in good soil, with deep roots to sustain them. How deep are the roots of your faith? Remember, your faith is not fragile, but resilient. What steps can you take to nurture this resilient connection with God that can withstand life's challenges?

Think about times when you felt distant or resistant to God's presence. How has He shown His love and faithfulness to you during those times? It's important to recognize and feel valued by His love. How can you open your heart to His comfort and guidance, even when facing frustration, disappointment, or doubt?

But He said to me, "My grace is sufficient for you, for my power is made perfect in weakness." Therefore I will boast all the more gladly about my weaknesses, so that Christ's power may rest on me.

—2 CORINTHIANS 12:9

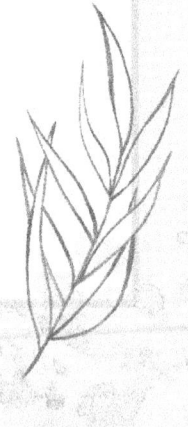

CHAPTER SIX

Meeting the Holy Spirit — Take Two

Trisha's Story

I bounced around a lot in my late teens and early twenties. Constantly feeling off-center, I never felt like I fit in anywhere. Right after high school, I found myself at Texas A&M Kingsville, where, in my floral dresses and Doc Martens, I looked very different from most students who wore Wrangler jeans and Justin boots. After two years, I transferred to the University of Texas at Austin and immediately fell in step with the city's laid-back cadence.

Austin was everything I had been looking for—dynamic, liberal, and welcoming to everyone. You could be a weirdo, a freak, a nerd, or a sweetheart. Everything paired well with Austin. And after spending the previous two years barely getting by emotionally, I was desperate to find a version of myself that I liked. I wanted to feel like a normal twenty-year-old. I longed to feel alive. And that's when cocaine found me. I was its perfect target.

One night, at a friend's house, I sat timidly against the coffee table and watched as a tray filled with cocaine made its way to me. I was still very insecure, afraid people could see through me and find my secret. But sitting knee to knee with new friends, people who felt as sunny as

Austin, I couldn't get up and leave. So, when it was my turn, I inhaled that thin, white line of powder with gusto. Almost immediately, I felt its powerful effects melt away all hesitation I had felt just seconds before. And an hour later, I had morphed into the most gorgeous social butterfly. There she was—the version of myself I had always wanted to be.

But of course, she wasn't real. As soon as the drug's spell wore off, I was back to being just plain, insecure me—and I couldn't stand that. So, after that night, I looked for any occasion to transform into the "better" me. For three years, I took my tonic whenever I could, growing addicted to the surge of confidence it gave. Soon, just a few lines wouldn't do. I needed more and more until, right around my twenty-third birthday, one of my best friends staged a mini-intervention.

"You need help. You're doing it more often and look awful," he told me. I could see that he was sincerely concerned, so my response was to stop hanging out with him.

But several months later, I experienced a different kind of intervention. It was a weeknight, and by then, I had all but stopped going to my classes. There were five of us crammed into a small one-bedroom apartment near the UT campus, each bringing enough cocaine to last all night. For eight hours straight, we inhaled line after line, not stopping until every last bit of it was gone.

The next morning, after everyone had found a corner to fall asleep, I sat anxiously, craving more. I was hot. My pulse was racing. *Maybe I can find some near campus.* With bloodshot eyes and sweat dripping from my brow, I gathered my things and walked out into the daylight. A few blocks from the apartment, I realized how incredibly dehydrated I was. I stumbled. People stared. I kept my eyes on the ground and moved forward.

As I approached Guadalupe Street, a sense of unease crept over me. I knew I had to rest before attempting to find a dealer. Buying drugs off the street was uncharted territory for me—I usually got my supply from a friend. I began to feel apprehensive, realizing I hadn't thought this through. As I stood there, hesitating, I could feel the stares multiplying as jitters moved through my body. My heart beat faster, my mouth ran dry, and I urgently needed water, shade, and rest. Afraid I was about to faint, I made my way toward the nearest building, leaned my cheek against the cold stone wall, and closed my eyes. Seconds later, I heard the jangle of keys unlocking a door but was too weak to lift my head or even open my eyes fully.

"Why don't you come inside?" a man said gently.

Without looking up, I felt the cool air from the doorway and shuffled toward it. As I stepped inside, I stopped and gasped. My surroundings came into focus. The man wasn't just any stranger—he was a priest. And I wasn't just anywhere—I was standing inside a simple but elegant church.

"Take a seat… and all the time you need," he said, motioning toward the pews.

I nodded and found my way to the front of the altar, and I knew… God had just saved my life.

Looking up above the altar at Jesus hanging from the cross, all the pain I had been experiencing seemed insignificant compared to what He had felt.

"I'm sorry, Jesus. I just don't know how to deal with this. I'm so sorry."

At that moment, I felt the hand of God, through the Holy Spirit, for the second time. And I understood. He had plans for me—a future and a hope just like the plaque in my parent's house declared. The first time I felt His presence reminded me that I wasn't alone. This time, it was a call to action—a chance to rebuild my life with God's grace.

After that experience, I stopped doing drugs, got myself into therapy, and slowly started to like myself again. It wasn't instant or easy, but every day after that, I leaned on God to get through the cravings, the guilt, and the overwhelming stress of not knowing what came next. He gave me strength as I rebuilt my life, one step at a time.

MEETING THE HOLY SPIRIT — TAKE TWO

Though buried under years of insecurity and poor choices, my faith had never truly left me. It had been there all along, quietly waiting for me to be ready for it to emerge. He had been guiding me even when I couldn't see it, and now, He was calling me back to the person I was meant to be.

REFLECTIONS

Think of a time when you were at a low point and needed a fresh start. How did God—or might He—invite you to begin again, and how did you respond?

Where in your life do you need healing or a new perspective? How could inviting the Holy Spirit to guide you through these challenges bring transformation?

When God offers us the chance to rebuild, He often asks us to let go of old patterns or choices that hold us back. What might God be prompting you to release, and how could surrendering this bring you closer to who He's calling you to be?

The Lord is close to the brokenhearted and saves those who are crushed in spirit.

—PSALM 34:18

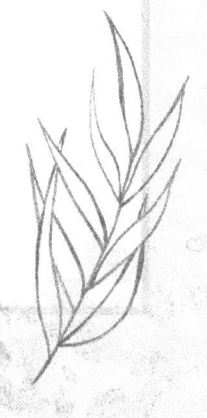

CHAPTER SEVEN
My Little Angel
Toni's Story

Disclaimer: This chapter addresses experiences of trauma, mental health struggles, and thoughts of self-harm. If you or someone you know is struggling, remember that help is available. You don't have to face this alone. Reach out to a mental health professional, a trusted friend, or call a support line. In the United States, you can call the National Suicide Prevention Lifeline at 988, available 24/7. In the UK, call 111. You are not alone; there is hope and help.

The struggles in my life never disappeared—they just took different forms. After my encounters with God and the Holy Spirit, I had hoped my life would finally smooth out. But the deeper wounds of my past, especially the trauma of my abuse, remained. I hadn't fully faced them, and over time, the scars I thought I'd buried began to surface in ways I couldn't ignore.

For years, I had pushed the memories down, as deeply as possible. Then, one day, a commercial about child abuse aired on TV, and it all came flooding back. The weight of it—the unprocessed pain—started seeping into my marriage and everyday life. Suddenly, I found myself shrinking back whenever David tried to hold me. My self-worth plummeted, leaving me feeling ugly, broken, and defeated. I was haunted by the thought that one day, my daughters would look at me and see a woman who couldn't find the courage to become the mother they truly deserved.

Desperation drove me to seek medical help. I was prescribed antidepressants and sleeping pills, but they only numbed my feelings. During the day, I felt like a zombie; at night, I stayed awake, dreading the nightmares. In my stupor, dark thoughts whispered: *Maybe my family, my precious girls, would be better off without me.*

The turning point came unexpectedly when my mom got sick. I decided to travel alone to San Antonio to visit her, and in a haze of sadness, I saw it as the perfect chance to end my pain. I wrote a letter to David, left it in a desk drawer, and made my plans. My mother-in-law came to stay with Trisha and Lisa, keeping them safe and cared for. I felt strangely at peace as if I had finally surrendered to the inevitable.

I made it to San Antonio, spent time with my mom, and said goodbye, forcing myself to act like everything was normal. But in my heart, I was preparing for the end. I bought a bottle of liquor and headed to my shabby motel room. Sitting on the edge of the bed, I gathered my pills and set everything on the nightstand. I was ready to go through with it. I was ready to end my life. But before I did, I wanted to hear my daughters' voices one last time.

When I called earlier that day, they were having too much fun playing to come to the phone. But listening to them in the background as I spoke to my mother-in-law was enough for me. I just wanted to hear their laughter one last time. I grabbed the phone and dialed. I felt anxious as I waited for my mother-in-law to pick up. But this time, to my surprise, Trisha answered.

"Hi, Mommy!" she said brightly, but before I could respond, she asked, "When are you coming home? We miss you so much." Her words hit me harder than I could have imagined. She added, "Lisa has been crying because she misses you."

A lump formed in my throat as I asked, "Aren't you having fun with Grandma?"

"Yes," she replied softly, "but we want you to come home."

Then my mother-in-law took the phone. Her tone was gentle but concerned as she explained that Lisa wouldn't stop asking for me. She had cried all night and even kept a picture of me under her pillow. Hearing those words, I felt my resolve waver, but I stubbornly clung to my decision.

In the background, Trisha shouted to her sister, "Lisa, Mommy's on the phone!"

I held my breath and soon heard my youngest daughter's sweet voice. Through her tears, she said, "Mommy, please come home. I need you. I miss you so much. Please come back."

The sound of her sobs broke me. As soon as I hung up the phone, I dropped to my knees, weeping as the enormity of what I had planned crushed me. How could I have been so blinded by my pain? Lisa was God's little angel, reaching out to pull me back from what I was about to do. I knew then that I couldn't go through with it. I flushed the pills and liquor down the toilet.

The next morning, I visited my mom again, then hurried home.

When I walked in, I was met by the arms of my daughters, who clung to me with such joy and relief that I felt a new resolve take root in my heart. I held them tight, not wanting to let go. I knew I needed real help and was finally ready to seek it.

I found a therapist who helped me work through the painful memories, the weight of years of trauma, and my self-blame. The journey wasn't easy, but I attended every appointment, took my medication, and even added exercise to my routine. Eventually, I realized none of these things could bring me the peace I needed most. I wanted to be whole—not just in mind and body, but in spirit. So, I returned to God, seeking the healing that only He could provide.

I began meeting regularly with a priest who guided me through the healing process with God at the center. In our sessions, the Holy Spirit worked through him, helping me confront the darkest parts of myself. Piece by piece, I unraveled, shedding years of bottled guilt and pain. He assigned me an exercise I'll never forget: to write letters to each person who had hurt me, expressing everything I had been holding inside. I poured it all out—anger, sadness, and heartbreak. Writing through tears, I filled pages, releasing years of disappointment and hurt.

Then, he gave me a new assignment: I had to write new letters, this time with the intent to forgive. He reminded me that forgiveness was a journey, not a destination, and that there was no deadline. He said, "When you're ready, God will let you know." With each prayer and each Scripture he recommended, I felt my heart soften. Finally, the time came. I went to the chapel, and in a quiet corner, I wrote a letter of forgiveness for each person who had hurt me. The memories were painful, but as I wrote, the weight on my heart gradually lifted.

But the most challenging assignment lay ahead. One day, my priest looked at me and said, "Now you must forgive yourself. You need to write a letter to Toni."

I stared at him, horrified at the thought. How could I forgive myself—not just for almost abandoning my family, but also for the cruel way I had treated myself?

He explained, "You've blamed Toni for everything bad that happened in your childhood. You've told her she's unworthy, unloved, and better off gone. You need to speak to her, tell her you're sorry, and let her know she is loved—by you, God, and everyone who cares for her."

I was overwhelmed. I tried to write the letter, but it was agony. My heart resisted the words, the forgiveness I so desperately needed to give. After countless drafts, tears, and prayers, I finally finished. In the letter, I told myself that I was a child of God, a daughter of the King, and worthy of love. Standing before a mirror with the letter in hand, I faced the reflection I had avoided for so long.

"I'm sorry," I whispered, and as the words tumbled out, everything I'd held back poured from my heart. I told myself I would care for her, cherish her, and treat her with the kindness she deserved. It felt like I was speaking to a long-lost friend, the most genuine part of myself.

At that moment, I felt surrounded by the love of God, as if His arms—and those of the Blessed Mother and the saints—were embracing me. I could almost hear the angels singing. It was a rebirth, the moment I let go and let God take over.

REFLECTIONS

How do you seek comfort and support in times of deep pain or struggle? Reflect on the people, practices, or beliefs that help you feel grounded. How might leaning on God or reaching out to others help you through difficult moments?

Self-forgiveness, a complex but vital part of healing, often requires a powerful motivator. What aspects of your life or past are proving to be stumbling blocks in your journey to forgiveness? Consider how God's unconditional love for you could be the driving force for you to show the same compassion and understanding to yourself.

Have you ever had a moment that reignited your sense of purpose or rekindled your hope? Reflect on the profound impact of that moment and how it reshaped your perspective or bolstered your resilience. Consider how seeking God's guidance and comfort could steer you towards peace and strength.

Trust in the Lord with all your heart and lean not on your own understanding; in all your ways submit to him, and he will make your paths straight.

—PROVERBS 3:5-6

CHAPTER EIGHT
My Perfect Life List
Trisha's Story

It was one of those cold yet sunny days in New York—a far cry from the hot, humid South Texas climate I left to pursue my career in television. The sky was clear, and the sun was bright, but condensation on the glass hinted at the chill outside. I looked out at the city that had been my home for years. It was stunning; no doubt about that. In the past, this view would have motivated and inspired me. But this day, the bright cityscape left me longing for something different—something I couldn't quite name.

New York had been part of my life for a long time, yet I never felt like it had become mine. When I met my husband, I told him that the city wasn't part of my long-term plan. I couldn't see myself raising children in New York. But each time I mentioned moving somewhere else, he argued that our rent-stabilized apartment was too good a deal to give up. I couldn't shake the feeling I was drifting further away from the life I was meant for. *Why can't I just be happy with what I have?*

I'd been promoted to Head of Content Strategy at MTV a few months earlier. I couldn't believe that my journey from intern to executive had brought me back to the same floor of the building where I'd started. It should've felt like a triumph; instead, I felt nothing. Sitting alone in that office, a strange emptiness pressed in from all sides.

I'd worked hard, yet my personal life seemed to be crumbling, and my work was unfulfilling. My depression had reached depths I hadn't known since my early twenties. Every day, my husband and I fought. Our pain turned us against each other, and I was exhausted from years of trying to fix our relationship. Still, I wasn't ready to face the hard truths I knew were coming. Hiding from my troubles, I'd pour myself a glass of wine each night to soothe my agitation. Then at work each day, I found comfort by daydreaming.

As I gazed at the rooftops below the window of my high-rise office, I wondered what kind of life I would choose if I could start over. I grabbed a scrap of paper from my desk and, without overthinking, scribbled down a list.

MY PERFECT LIFE:

- I speak Spanish fluently.
- I live someplace warm, with palm trees.
- I live somewhere with a large Hispanic community—I want to be with my people.
- I live in a cute, cottage-like home.
- I have a daughter.
- I'm doing something creative with my life.
- I'm making a difference in the world (small or large).
- I see my family often.
- I continue to explore—to constantly seek.
- I exercise, eat well, and take care of myself.
- I love myself.

When I finished writing, I took a step back and felt a jolt of surprise. Since when did I want to learn Spanish so badly? But as I reread the list,

I remembered that it had been a long-buried goal of mine to speak with my grandmother, who'd never learned English, in her own language. As for living somewhere warm, with palm trees... that one didn't surprise me at all. The rest, though, seemed like a pipe dream. I was so firmly planted in the life I'd created that living any other way felt impossible. Uproot my life? No, I'd worked too hard. But at that moment, though I didn't realize it, God was beginning to work in me. I had no way of knowing then, but each line was pointing me toward a life that God, in His perfect wisdom, was already preparing.

Seven months later, my world was unrecognizable. My marriage had ended, and I lost my job. Alone in an unfurnished apartment in the West Village, I found myself unpacking the scattered remnants of what had once been my life—office boxes mingled with those from the home I'd shared with my husband. I sat on the hard floor, wondering if I was building a new life or dismantling the old one. I couldn't decide which felt worse.

In those first weeks, I did little more than sit, drink, and stare out the window, hoping somehow my life would take shape again. I couldn't bring myself to organize the boxes stacked around me. They held too many reminders of everything I'd recently lost. But one afternoon, feeling desperate to take a step forward, I rummaged through a box from my office. The paper with my "Perfect Life" list was mixed in with various binders and folders.

Seeing it again, crumpled at the bottom, I felt a strange mix of sorrow and hope. For a moment, I didn't know whether to laugh or cry. I was surrounded by boxes of what felt like my entire life packed away—and here was this list, a part of me that obviously wanted to be found. I read each line slowly. Now, instead of feeling like an unobtainable wish list, it felt like a secret message.

MY PERFECT LIFE LIST

In a strange way, finding it reignited something in me. It didn't erase the sadness, but it did bring a hint of clarity. Maybe, just maybe, I needed to start over somewhere new, closer to the life I envisioned. A few months later, I packed up and left New York for Barcelona, following a pull I couldn't explain. At the time, though I wouldn't admit it, I thought I was fleeing, trying to escape the shame of failure. But looking back now, I realize that even then, God had been gently guiding me toward something greater, using that list to point me forward.

When I arrived in Spain, though I was depressed and broken, a part of me knew I had to lose everything to become the person He wanted me to be. Still, the way forward wasn't clear, and that frustrated me. After about a year abroad, I decided to move back to the States, where life felt more predictable. Then COVID-19 hit, and it felt like God was forcing my hand again. I had no choice but to stay put.

After the pandemic ended, with a newfound appreciation for freedom (and adventure), I decided to give Spain another go. I moved from Barcelona to Madrid for a fresh perspective and quickly joined the expat community. As soon as travel felt safe again, I flew back to Texas to visit my family—and finally sign my divorce papers.

I hadn't been to my parents' house in years, not since before I moved to Spain. All my boxes had been sent there for storage, piled haphazardly in their spare bedroom. An entire era of my life had been packed into enough cardboard to fill a small room. The process of reorganizing was torture. Categorizing everything into "keep" or "throw" took me weeks; I could only handle the emotional toll in small doses. But just as I neared the finish line, the list found me again.

A few things had already come true in the years since I'd first written those words. I was now able to speak to my grandma in her native language. My Spanish was far from perfect, but I felt so proud when I saw the joy in her face when we talked. I was living in Madrid, the epicenter of Hispanic culture. And though not plentiful like in other areas of Spain, palm trees dotted the city.

There was a lot on my Perfect Life list that I still didn't have, but those things no longer felt out of reach. I was moving closer to the life I'd once only dreamed of. It was a reminder that I hadn't been alone on this journey—God had been guiding me, even when I felt lost. The list became more than just wishes on a page. It reflected the person God was calling me to be, a treasure map leading me, step by step, toward a life I hadn't fully understood but now could see with new eyes. I realized that my dreams, even the ones I hadn't spoken aloud, were known by God. Each time it reappeared, it was like a future version of myself was urging me to trust the path ahead. In time, I saw that the journey was less about achieving a "perfect" life and more about surrendering to a life where I could fully embrace His plans for me.

Even now, I hold onto that list as a reminder of God's perfect timing—that He knows the desires of our hearts, even when we can't see the whole picture. The words on that page remain a touchstone, pointing me back to the truth that each step I take, even the painful ones, is leading me toward the life He has always intended for me.

REFLECTIONS

Think about a time when you felt you were living a life that didn't align with who you truly are. What emotions did that disconnect bring up for you? If you could make a 'perfect life' list today, what would you include to move closer to a life that reflects your deepest desires?

Have you ever rediscovered something—a goal, a passion, or even an old journal—that felt like a reminder of who you want to become? What was it, and how did it impact the decisions you made afterward?

Are there dreams or aspirations you've set aside, thinking they were unrealistic or unattainable? Consider revisiting them now. What steps, even small ones, could you take to align your current path with these dreams? How might God be gently guiding you toward them?

I will give you a new heart and put a new spirit in you; I will remove from you your heart of stone and give you a heart of flesh.

—EZEKIEL 36:26

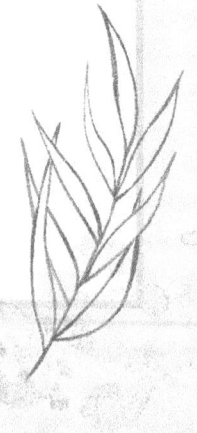

CHAPTER NINE
A Christmas Miracle
Toni's Story

Twenty years ago, an extraordinary event shocked the residents of the Rio Grande Valley, a region in the southernmost part of Texas along the Mexican border. For my family, what happened became a marker in our lives: who we were before the snow and who we became afterward. Our lives were transformed, but our story actually began months earlier, in March 2004.

My husband, David, had been feeling worn out for weeks. Every day, he'd come home from work and go straight to bed, but I was too consumed by my grief to notice. Just a month earlier, my sister, Gloria, died, and I was devastated. She was the first of my siblings to pass away, and it hurt me deeply. I woke up in pain and went to sleep in pain. She had been more than a big sister—she had been my best friend and the person in my family I talked to the most about God. I could tell Gloria anything, and I knew she would listen without judgment. I loved her so much, but then she was gone.

So, when David's behavior started to change —the early Saturday mornings washing the cars and the hours spent in his garden were gone— I really didn't notice. Looking back, I feel guilty for not realizing the problem's seriousness. It wasn't until he told me that he needed to see a doctor that I felt a familiar dread simmering in the pit of my stomach.

"Babe, I think something's wrong," he said one evening. "With everything you're going through, I didn't want to worry you, but something's not right."

"What do you mean?" I asked him in an almost accusing tone. "David, tell me."

"I've been really tired lately, and it's getting worse," he began. I could see in his eyes that he was trying not to scare me. "Maybe it's a vitamin deficiency or something. Whatever it is, I think I should go to my doctor and have him check it out."

Perhaps it was a push from above—from Gloria—but something inside me snapped. This was important.

"Make the appointment now, babe. Let's not wait," I told him, speaking calmly but urgently.

David and I had been together since we were teenagers, building a life and family from nothing but love and faith. When we got married, we were naïve—but determined. And from the beginning, we welcomed God into our union. On our wedding day, as soon as we walked out of the courthouse, I took David's hand and led him toward the San Fernando Cathedral just across the street.

"We should go ask the priest for a blessing," I said eagerly. He smiled in agreement, and feeling my heart swell with love, I knew I had just made the right decision to marry him. Even though everyone said we were too young and that we'd never last, I knew in my heart that we were meant to be.

We were surprised to find no one else inside as we stepped into the cathedral. Still, we walked timidly to the altar, treading lightly like mischievous children sneaking into their parents' room. Just as we reached the altar, a priest came around the corner and saw us.

"Good morning," he said, his voice cheerful. "Can I help you with something?"

"Father, this is my new wife," David said proudly as I blushed. "We just came from the courthouse. But we need God's blessing before we start our life together."

The priest smiled warmly and motioned us to move closer to him. Standing there, I knew we would face whatever life brought our way, side by side.

Now, decades later, we were confronted with a challenge unlike any we'd ever faced. A few days after David shared his concerns, he saw our primary care doctor. David's fatigue, shortness of breath, and swollen ankles concerned the doctor enough to refer him to a cardiologist.

The cardiologist scheduled a series of tests, including an echocardiogram and a cardiac catheterization, to better understand what was happening with David's heart. I sat alone in the cardiologist's office, waiting for my husband to come out of the recovery room, gripping my chair, desperate for answers. I can still remember the stoic look on the doctor's face when he told me the news.

"Congestive heart failure," he explained, his face expressionless. "He'll live two, maybe four years at best—but only if he gets a heart transplant."

"What? What do you mean?" My voice was shrill with frantic urgency.

"It's not all doom and gloom," he quickly added, as if those words would be any help. How could he talk about David's life as if two to four more years could ever be enough?

I don't remember walking down the hallway after that. Somehow, I made it to David's room. As soon as I walked in, he looked up at me, and with tears running down his face, he said, "I'm sorry we won't grow old together."

I shattered. *Not my husband, too. God, please.*

He was quiet for a moment, then repeated it. "I'm sorry."

In that moment, the life we'd built and the future we'd always imagined felt like they were slipping away. I scooted up next to him and held onto him tighter than ever.

Those first days after the diagnosis were a blur. We were numb, submitting to the prognosis we'd been given. Soon, David began to hand out instructions for when he was gone, talking about IRAs and life insurance. But I couldn't listen to any of it. *I'm not ready to be a widow.*

However, a few days later, when our daughters flew in from New York, the energy in the house shifted.

"Mom, you can't listen to the first doctor you meet. We're going to get a second opinion," Trisha told me, determined and resolute.

But I still wasn't ready to move from heartbroken to hopeful. Instead, I cried in my room, feeling like I was losing too much—first Gloria, now David. I was livid. *This isn't fair, Lord.*

"Hey, Mom." I heard Lisa's voice through the door. She sounded concerned.

"Yeah, Mija. I'm okay," I shouted back.

"Can I come in?" she asked. Hearing the tension in her voice, I realized my daughters were in pain, too. I couldn't make David's illness all about me.

"Of course," I replied.

But instead of seeing tears in Lisa's eyes when she opened the door, I saw empathy. She walked over and hugged me, holding me as fiercely as I had held David the day we got the diagnosis. When convinced I wouldn't fall apart, she looked at me and said, "Mom, where's your faith?" She didn't mean it as a rebuke but as a reminder. And something in me shifted. *Yes,* I thought. *Where is my faith?*

With our daughters' help, we got a second opinion. But it was the third, from a specialist at the DeBakey Heart Center in Houston, that slowly changed things for us.

"I'm sorry I don't have better news," the doctor said sincerely. "But you know, we're not throwing in the towel either. There are things we can try to lessen the strain on his heart. But these aren't cures. For that, we're talking heart transplant; but let's take one thing at a time."

Though we had wished for a different outcome, the care David received in Houston gave him a little bit of hope. And with that hope came brief bursts of energy. That summer, we agreed when some friends invited us to travel with them to the Shrine of the Most Blessed Sacrament in Alabama.

When we arrived, I could see that David was hesitant to climb the stairs up to the main entrance.

"You up to this?" I asked. "If it's too hot or you're feeling weak, we can wait for them down here."

David shook his head. It didn't matter to him that the heat from the bright rays of the midday sun could quickly make even a fit eighteen-year-old tire.

"We came all this way," he said. "I'm doing it. I'm going up."

And slowly, he did.

When we reached the top of the stairs, an outline of a statue stood against the bright sky. We stopped to rest in the small patch of shade it offered, finally averting our eyes from the sun. As the statue came into view, we both gasped.

"Babe, it's baby Jesus, and look at His hand," I exclaimed. "He's holding a heart."

Standing in front of the statue of the Divine Child with His Sacred Heart exposed and His hand outstretched, David's eyes filled with tears. I squeezed his arm and whispered, "Look, His other hand is in His chest. That's His Heart He's holding. He's going to give it to you." David fell to his knees and wept. Our little sprig of hope blossomed into a full bouquet at that moment.

But that fall, at one of his monthly check-ups, David's doctors pushed us. He wasn't getting any better, and we needed to get him on the transplant list. We hesitantly agreed. That night, I prayed with all my might that David would get a new heart soon. Now that he was on the list, it suddenly felt like an hourglass had been placed on the table. Urgency grew with every grain of sand that slid from the top of the glass to the bottom. So, my prayers grew more insistent, too. *Let David get to the top of the transplant list soon,* I begged.

But a month later, as we sat in the waiting room, I heard a woman ask the man beside her, "How old is yours?"

"Forty-two," he replied. "And yours?"

"Twenty-eight," she said, placing her hand on her chest.

Then the realization hit—they were talking about their hearts. *The person who died was only twenty-eight, Trisha's age.* Immediately, a wave of nausea washed over me. I had been praying this whole time for another to die so that my husband could live.

That night, my petition to God changed. "God, I don't want You to give David someone else's heart…I need You to heal *his* heart," I said. "I know You can do it. You can move mountains, part seas. You are the Lord. You can heal David's heart. I believe, Lord. I believe."

That November, our friends Annette and Arnold came to pray over David, along with Annette's parents, Rosa and Joe. Rosa and Joe were charismatic and energetic, and as they prayed over David, their commanding voices boomed throughout the house. I closed my eyes, feeling the presence of something far beyond the walls of our home. As our prayers grew louder and more insistent, the room felt like it was vibrating. And when I opened my eyes to look at David, he had a strange expression. He was dazed, as if he didn't know where he was. Suddenly, he collapsed. When we got him up, he stared at us with a strange, peaceful curiosity.

"David, are you okay?" I asked.

He nodded "yes" before sitting back down.

"What happened?" I pressed.

"I don't know," he whispered. "I can't... I can't describe it."

Because of the tranquility in his eyes, I knew—God had sent the Holy Spirit into our home, and David was healed. From that night on, I again changed my prayers. Instead of pleading, "Please heal him," I said, "Thank You, Jesus. Thank You for healing him." My heart felt lighter knowing that God had lifted the burden of worry from me.

But even though I knew David was healed, I still wanted a sign.

"God, I'm sorry to ask, but I just need something to let me know You are with us." Then I shrugged and added, "I'm sorry, but You made me this way. You know I always ask for signs."

Just then, a thought popped into my head. Snow.

Snow, God?

Snow seemed impossible in the Rio Grande Valley, known for its palm trees and citrus groves. McAllen, the town where we lived, was even coined the "City of Palms" because there were so many of them. Winter didn't exist in this part of Texas. Snow had only fallen once in the past hundred years, and even then, it was just a light dusting. The idea of snow on Christmas felt too big, as if I was asking for something ridiculous. But I couldn't shake it.

"Okay, God, maybe you can send me just a little flurry a month from now?" I hesitantly asked. "I will take one flurry—one little snowflake to let me know You're here."

In my excitement, I began to tell everyone that David had been healed but was usually met with dubious looks.

"Healed, Toni?" my friend Crawford would tease. "And snow? On Christmas? Here?"

As Christmas inched closer, I held onto my faith. But on December 21st, when Trisha and Lisa arrived for the holiday, they were greeted with a clear, sunny sky.

"I'm sorry, Mom," Trisha said as she hugged me. "When we landed, the pilot said it was 82 degrees."

"Yeah, but it's okay," I cheerfully replied. "I heard this morning that a cold front is coming." Both of my girls looked at me like I was crazy. I knew it was hard for them to trust that their dad would be okay. They were worried about him—and about me. Now, they thought I had created a different reality because I was unable to cope with the thought of losing David. But I couldn't let their doubts affect me.

The next day, December 22nd, the temperatures dropped down to the low 40's, and a handful of friends began calling.

"Wow, Toni, it's getting cold," exclaimed Crawford. "But nothing about snow in the forecast."

"Not yet," I corrected him. "And all I need is one single snowflake."

The following day, the 23rd, though the temperature had dropped slightly, it was still hovering in the high thirties—too warm to make snow. I was clutching onto optimism, but the house's melancholy atmosphere started weighing on me. David had gone to bed with a fever and a cough. The rattle in his breathing startled me, and I watched him sleep all night. I needed to see his chest move with each inhale and exhale.

It wasn't until early in the morning that I forced myself downstairs to make a pot of coffee. With my mug filled, I went to the living room to pray. *I'm sorry, Lord, for feeling so scared. I promise, I do believe. It's just that seeing him this way is so hard.* Just then, I heard the shuffle of feet coming down the stairs.

"Hey," I heard Trisha say. "Dad?"

"No, Mijita, it's me." My voice broke as I answered, and I realized I'd been crying. *God, give me strength.*

I don't know whether it was the lack of sleep or the gloominess of a silent house, but that morning, I couldn't pretend that the past year hadn't taken its toll on me. I missed Gloria, and with David's diagnosis, I hadn't yet given her death the space it deserved. So, when I found myself alone on quiet mornings, I surrendered to the pain of losing my sister.

As Trisha and I sat in silence, lost in the Christmas tree's blinking lights, I heard her say, "Mom, is it raining... on Christmas Eve?"

I sat still and listened. It was drizzling. *Oh, Lord, forgive me. You've been by my side this whole time.*

Later, while David and Trisha, who was now also feeling sick, were napping, Lisa kept a close watch on the weather.

"Mom, hurry," Lisa shouted from the living room. "Tim Smith's back on." Her voice boomed over Channel Five's meteorologist.

"Put it louder," I screamed excitedly as I rushed by her side.

"Now, I don't want to get y'all too excited," he began. "But, if the temperatures drop just a few more degrees, we *might* see some wintry precipitation," he said cautiously. "So, if you're gonna be out on the roads, be careful because they'll likely be slick with rain *and* sleet."

"I'm gonna run up to tell Dad and Trish," Lisa said, her face flushed with excitement. "Too bad they're not feeling well. They're missing all the action."

A few hours later, as Lisa and I left Mass, we saw that the rain had started to mix with tiny flecks of ice. I held my hand out and watched as heavy drops fell and quickly melted. Smiling, I turned to Lisa, then looked up at the sky.

"They might be melting down here, but somewhere up there, there's gotta be at least one little snowflake," I said with complete confidence. But throughout the night, as I waited for the sleet to turn a shade of white, it never happened. *It's okay, God. I know somewhere in all this rain, You sent me my snowflake.*

Just before ten o'clock, with heavy lids, I thought about heading upstairs for bed. The rain had started falling intermittently, and I was content with the sign God had sent me earlier that day. But then I heard Tim Smith say, "Folks, you're not going to believe this. With the temperature now below freezing, we're getting reports of snow flurries out at McAllen International Airport."

"Did... did he say?" Lisa stuttered.

Before I could answer, she zipped upstairs to tell Trisha the news. Soon, both girls huddled around me, and the three of us watched the night sky carefully.

"Should we wake up Dad?" Trisha asked.

I shook my head. I wanted to wait until there was something *real* to tell him.

"I think I saw a flake," Lisa called out excitedly from her post by the sliding door, and I jumped to my feet.

"Put your coat on first," was all I could say, my heart racing with anticipation.

I don't remember running to the door, only standing outside, looking up at the stars. Above me, delicate white flakes drifted from the sky. The world was still and calm, wrapped in a holy silence. I was speechless. Soon, the little specks grew into larger puffs, and the ground turned a powdery white. I laughed. And danced. And thanked the Lord.

Our entire world had transformed the following day when we all stepped outside. Snow had fallen throughout the night, and the whole neighborhood was covered. Little did I know then, but the entire region was blanketed in snow, soft and thick, unlike anything we had ever seen. The sight of palm trees draped in white, their leaves bowing down under the snow's weight, will never leave me. I stood there, marveling at this miracle, this gift that covered our home. It was a sight I never imagined, but there they were—bending palms, announcing God's Christmas miracle.

The sign I'd prayed for had arrived—a gift in the stillness of the night that filled my heart with gratitude. Twenty years have passed since then. David and I celebrated our fiftieth anniversary this past May, renewing our vows in the same cathedral where we first prayed together and asked God to bless our lives. We've grown in our faith together, with David even becoming a deacon, a path he felt called to after that snowy Christmas.

Sometimes, I still wake up in the quiet hours, watching his chest rise and fall with the soft rhythm of his breathing. I reach for his hand, feeling its warmth, and say a quiet prayer of thanks. That snowfall twenty years ago was just one of many miracles we've witnessed in our lives, each a reminder of God's endless love and mercy. And with every miracle, it felt as though He was saying, "I am here, even when you can't see Me, even in the impossible."

REFLECTIONS

When have you witnessed God's presence in a surprising or miraculous way? How did it impact your faith or change the way you see Him?

Think about an area in your life where you feel the need for a sign or reassurance. How could you open your heart to see the subtle ways God might already be working there?

What does trust in God's timing look like for you? How might you embrace waiting or uncertainty as an invitation to grow closer to Him?

But those who hope in the Lord will renew their strength. They will soar on wings like eagles; they will run and not grow weary, they will walk and not be faint.

—ISAIAH 40:31

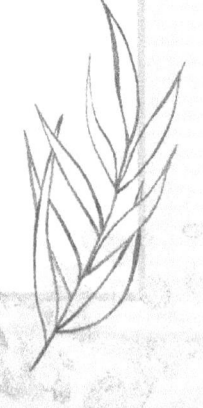

CHAPTER TEN
The Companion on the Camino
Trisha's Story

In my apartment, with the blinds lowered, I sat alone in blackness. My body was battered—my foot swollen, my back aching, and my hand clumsily wrapped in bandages from a fall in the shower. I tried to feel a connection to God, but He was nowhere to be found. Good thing I came back home when I did; otherwise, I might've ended up like Moses—wandering in the desert for the next forty years.

But as I sat there in silence, I found my mind drifting back to the Camino. Back to all the planning, packing, and research... back to the moment I thought I had finally figured everything out. I meticulously planned every detail of my Camino—backpacks, shoes, places to eat and sleep, even the best electrolytes to pack. I arranged weekly rest days, so I'd be able to physically sustain the 500-mile hike. I packed protein bars, a chafe stick, Compeed band-aids, and alcohol wipes. I downloaded self-help books and podcasts. I was confident I'd have my life completely figured out by the end of my 40-day trek. *But no... that would've been too easy, right, God?*

On my second day on the Camino de Santiago, I woke up to a bolt of searing pain shooting through my leg. My plantar fasciitis had flared up after the long hike over the Pyrenees. I could barely step out of bed, and I still had six weeks of hiking ahead of me. What I'd envisioned as a peaceful, reflective walk turned into a daily struggle, hobbling from village to village in excruciating pain. Too preoccupied with just trying to survive, I quickly abandoned the notion of "finding myself" and instead spent all my time finding ice. Once again, I was furious with God. I was trying to get my life together. I had everything planned out perfectly. Why, after all my good intentions, was He making it so hard for me?

I was swept up in a whirlpool of emotions—disoriented, disheartened, and *pissed*. One night, while blowing off steam with a group of Germans, the evening seemed typical enough. It wasn't unusual to dine and stay up late with fellow pilgrims. But as the night ended, I realized one of the guys was following me back to my hotel. Drunk, exhausted, and terrified, I ran to the hotel's front door. Once safely inside, I found my room, bolted the door, and stepped into the shower. I needed to wash off the ick from the night. But as soon as the warm water touched my skin, I broke down, sobbing and screaming at God. "I had a plan, God!" I shouted, and I knew I wasn't just talking about the Camino. At that moment, I slipped, cutting myself as I fell to the floor. Watching the blood flow from the gashes in my hand and swirl down the drain, I made a decision.

That was it. I was done.

The next morning, I packed my things and returned to Madrid, isolating myself to reckon with the pain on *my* terms.

"Mom, I made it to León. That's good enough," I told her over the phone while lounging on my sofa. "I basically did, like, seventy-five percent of the Camino. I'm good, right?"

Mom was silent.

"Well?" I pushed.

"Mija, the decision is up to you," she began. "If you can't finish the Camino, your dad and I aren't going to be disappointed in you. You did a lot more than most people."

Even though her words were supportive, there was something in her voice. It wasn't a lack of support—more like... a challenge.

"Yeah, I want to finish the Camino; I just can't," I said in a huff. "It's physically impossible. I have a busted foot, a wobbly knee, a jacked-up back. And now, I have a bandaged-up hand."

But after twenty minutes of listening to me outline all the reasons why going back on the Camino would be the worst idea ever, Mom stopped me. "Trisha, there's obviously something inside of you that you aren't paying attention to."

"What?" I asked, confused. "Well, what am I supposed to do?"

"Pray on it."

I rolled my eyes, frustrated. That wasn't the answer I wanted. I was hoping for a roadmap, a clear plan, a solution that didn't involve me risking my sanity all over again. Still, there was something in her voice—a quiet confidence that wouldn't let me shake the thought.

I couldn't see it then, but that moment was the start of a different kind of journey—one that wasn't about my physical pain, or my plans, or my control. It was a journey that would slowly teach me to let go, to trust, even when nothing made sense.

The next few days passed in a fog. I avoided the thought of returning to the Camino, distracting myself with Netflix and excuses. I kept telling myself it was a terrible idea. *It's too late. It's physically impossible. You've already proven enough.* But the more I tried to silence the nagging pull, the louder it became.

I thought I was the one figuring things out—me, alone. God and I had an on-again, off-again relationship, and let's be honest, it was mostly off-again. Sure, I'd talk to Him in passing, but when it came to big decisions, I was the one in charge. This time, though, I didn't know what to do.

So, for the first time in a long time, I let Him decide—I took Mom's advice and prayed. It wasn't a beautiful, poetic prayer like you'd hear in church. It was raw and messy, with a lot of *"What do you want from me?"* and *"If this is what You want, You're gonna have to make it clear because I don't see a way forward."*

The message I got was undeniable. I needed to go back. Even though I was apprehensive, I knew it wasn't my voice or my idea. Something bigger was at work, and I couldn't ignore it.

Days later, I found myself standing once again on the Camino, clutching my walking stick. The first few days were brutal. My foot ached relentlessly, and every step felt like walking over a bag of jagged rocks. But I kept going. It wasn't just about finishing what I'd started anymore. It was about facing the things I'd been running from long before I ever set foot in Spain.

By the third day back, the pain in my foot had settled to a six out of ten— manageable, though uncomfortable. But that morning, it shot back up to an eight. Every step sent sharp, stabbing jolts through my leg.

Staring at a church ahead, I watched two other pilgrims walk out, looking rested and refreshed. *It's open. Should I go in and relax for a bit?* My instincts told me to stop. But when I glanced up at the dark clouds gathering overhead, I made a different choice: better to get to the next town before the storm hit.

I dug my walking stick into the ground and pushed off with renewed strength. *Keep moving,* I told myself. But as I approached the church's perimeter, a man I hadn't noticed before stepped toward me.

"¿Quieres...?" he asked as he walked up to me. But aside from *'quieres,'* I had no idea what else he said.

"No, gracias," I muttered as I tried to pick up my pace to pass him.

"Pero..."

Again, I couldn't understand anything after *"but."* Though my Spanish was decent, there were certain accents that I had a hard time understanding. And the mask he was wearing over his mouth wasn't helping. So, I just gave him a meek smile and shrugged.

"Ah, English?"

Darn it.

"You.... Eh... You... Eh... ¿Cómo se dice?"

I didn't want to stop, but something in his eyes made me pause, a look that was both urgent and calm. *What did this man need?*

"Hablo un poco de Español, pero tienes que hablar *muyyy* lento ¿Vale?" When he heard me, his eyes lit up.

"You, no Spanish good," he replied. And I got the sense he was very proud of himself for speaking in English. "Yo hablo muy slow."

"¿Quieres rezar conmigo?" he asked, each word coming out lazily, like molasses.

He wants me to do what with him? My mind scrambled for the meaning, pulling on the bits of Spanish I knew. *Rezar. Rezar. Rezar.*

Seeing I was struggling to understand him, he took something gold from his coat pocket. Immediately, I assumed he was trying to sell me something.

"No, gracias. No, gracias," I said, waving my hand. But just as I was about to turn, I saw that he was holding a rosary.

"¿Rezar?" he said softly, then clasped his palms together in the universal symbol of prayer.

Ah, he wants me to pray the rosary with him. Looking up at the darkening sky and then back at him, I hesitated but knew I had no choice.

"Sí, claro que sí," I agreed.

But rather than stand and pray together, the man asked if he could walk with me. I nodded.

Taking turns saying the rosary in English and Spanish, we were about five minutes in before I realized he was limping.

Seeing him struggling, I told him, "No tenemos que caminar." I was happy to stand and pray. He didn't have to walk with me.

But he shook his head. "No, estoy bien," he said. "Díos me quita el dolor de la pierna cuando rezo." He then smiled broadly.

God takes away his pain when he prays.

As we both continued, hobbling along at a slow, easy pace, I found it hard to concentrate—his words lingered. *They had been meant just for me.* I knew it. And looking at the man beside me, I knew that was Jesus walking with me, working through him.

I bowed my head and cried softly.

"I will take away your pain." I heard the words clearly, and I knew Jesus wasn't just talking about my physical pain.

Fifteen minutes later, when we finished, the man put a piece of paper in my hand. It was a copy from pages of his prayer book.

"Vengo aquí todos los días y les pido a los peregrinos que recen conmigo," he began.

"Every day, you come out here and ask pilgrims to pray with you?" I asked, wanting to confirm I understood him.

"Yes," he said, nodding excitedly. "Pero no personas quieren. But you—yes. ¿Por qué?"

Looking back at him, I didn't have an answer. I didn't know why I had stopped. I just knew that I had to.

He hugged me with a kind, knowing look and then said, "You know. Acéptalo."

Almost seven hours later, I finally arrived in the next town. I had covered eighteen miles that day, but I promise you—when I took off my boots that night, my pain level was back down to a three.

And for the rest of the Camino, I prayed every single day... all the way to the Cathedral of Santiago de Compostela.

REFLECTIONS

Think about a journey you're currently on, whether physical, emotional, or spiritual. Where might God invite you to let go of control and trust Him with the path ahead?

On the Camino, the process itself became transformative. How could embracing the process—rather than just focusing on the destination—change your perspective in areas where you seek answers?

The Rosary became a source of strength and peace during this pilgrimage. What practice, prayer, or ritual might help you reconnect with God in moments of challenge or uncertainty?

Trust in the Lord with all your heart and lean not on your own understanding; in all your ways submit to him, and he will make your paths straight.

—PROVERBS 3:5-6

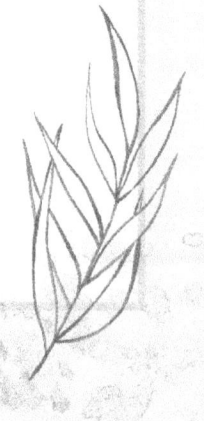

CHAPTER ELEVEN
Sweet Lord Divine
Trisha's Story

After finishing the Camino, I expected my life to change—but I wasn't sure how. My grand plan to walk away with a clear roadmap for my future had failed spectacularly. But one thing had become clear: the person I wanted to become. If I focused on becoming the woman God intended me to be, I trusted *she* would know what to do next.

Slowly, I let go of the need to "figure it all out" and embraced the idea that I'd recognize the path when it appeared. Sitting on the sofa and agonizing over my future wasn't going to get me anywhere. So, I began to step outside my comfort zone and explore. Some things felt right—others didn't at all.

Around this time, women in Madrid's expat community began reaching out to me for business advice, drawn by my corporate background. But I knew little about entrepreneurship, and most of these women were seeking guidance for their small businesses—even after I made it clear I wasn't an expert in that field. Still, they kept coming. They explained they were creatives who had never even written a business plan. They had spent their lives nurturing different skills than I had. They told me they needed strategy, organization, and accountability—areas where I knew I could offer support.

So, I helped, free of charge, until I realized what I was doing could grow into a business. However, a pattern became clear after just a few sessions with these women. What started as tactical meetings always turned into pep talks. They were making excuses for not following through on tasks they had committed to completing—and now they were beating themselves up for it. Drawing on my own experiences, I offered as much insight and support as I could—but it wasn't enough. I knew I needed to do better.

Overcome with a desire to help these women change behaviors that were stifling them, I looked into becoming a certified business coach. Surely, I wasn't the first to need professional development in this field. But the more I looked at programs and the different kinds of coaching certifications, the more I realized that, while I adored these women, I couldn't identify with them. At least, not yet. I had never launched a business. But coaching women in corporate who were now where I was five, ten, fifteen years ago? *That* I could do.

When I began researching coaching programs, I had no doubt I was meant to be an executive coach for minority women. I *knew* those women. I understood their struggles, and I was passionate about helping them. I'd found my calling.

With determination, I jumped into all things coaching. I got certified in both life coaching and executive coaching, launched my business, and flew out to New York with a calendar full of executive meetings. I was ready—eager. But within hours of landing, I received an email. Meeting canceled. Then another. And another. Soon, my entire trip unraveled; every meeting was canceled, and just like that, the busy itinerary I had built my expectations around dissolved.

Frustrated, I arrived back in Madrid feeling defeated and uncertain. What was all of this supposed to mean? I had poured myself into building a career as an executive coach, yet with just a few emails, it felt like all my efforts had been crushed.

Making it worse was the office. Just before I left for New York, I had leased an unfurnished private office, convinced it was the next step in my future. I was so excited, sure that God had opened this door for me—that finding that office was a sign I was on the right track. I'd imagined returning with signed contracts in hand, ready to make it official. Now, that vision felt like it was slipping away.

I couldn't stop thinking about how it all started. The morning I found the office had felt almost serendipitous. It had been a day like any other. I woke up and instinctively grabbed my phone. But as the screen lit up, a random "memory" from eight years earlier appeared—a photo of me sitting happily in my fancy new corner office at MTV. As I stared at the picture and then glanced at the tiny Ikea desk just a few feet from my bed, a wave of sadness washed over me. *What happened to that woman?*

But just as quickly as the thought entered my mind, I pushed it away. I was still that woman, wasn't I? And now I was better—more experienced, more focused. If the Trisha from eight years ago had an office, I deserved one, too. Before I'd even had my morning coffee, I'd contacted a realtor and made an appointment to see a space later that day.

I was shocked when she told me the address. It was just a few minutes' walk from my apartment—perfect. When I arrived, it felt like stepping into another era. The building was immaculate, a preserved 19th-century treasure with original details that felt almost untouched by time. The realtor, Begoña, ushered me inside and led me through the suite of offices.

"It's the last door at the end of the hall—the corner one," she said. I grinned. *Of course, it is.*

As soon as I stepped inside, the soaring sixteen-foot ceilings immediately caught my attention, making the space feel much larger than it was. The hardwood floors, intricate moldings, and a charming Juliet balcony gave the office an air of elegance, even though it was completely empty. I was drawn to it instantly, but the cost of furnishing the space gave me pause—until I noticed the view.

Approaching the balcony, I glimpsed part of the street and the building across through the wooden shutters. When I stepped outside, I was stunned. Directly in front of me stood the 17th-century church I had passed countless times before. I'd admired it from the street but hadn't realized the office would offer such a breathtaking perspective. A sense of peace washed over me as I stood there, taking it all in.

"I'd like to submit an application," I told Begoña eagerly.

"Just like that? Don't you want to see more offices?"

Once I'd convinced her that it wouldn't be necessary, she gave me a list of the documents she needed from me, including paystubs from the past three months.

"Can I just send you bank statements? I'm on a student visa and can't work in Spain," I replied.

"Oh, no. We require a work contract," she said sternly.

"Is that an absolute rule? Because I am launching a business now. It's just that it will be based in the U.S.," I told her, my voice full of pride and excitement. "I think this office has called me. I know I'm supposed to be here."

She gave a deep sigh before replying, "Okay, but we need to ask la Madre Maria."

"Mother Mary? We need to pray?" I asked, incredulous.

"No, no," she managed between laughs. "La Madre María is the head nun at the monastery next door. She will be your landlady."

Relieved I wouldn't have to kneel and pray in front of my realtor, I took a deep breath.

"Whew. Oh, good. You scared me," I told her. "If that's the case, I feel confident she's gonna say yes. Let's just say, I gotta good feeling about this."

Two days later, I was sitting across from Mother Mary, signing the contract.

But now, a month later, sitting on the floor among an assortment of boxes—all my furniture that had arrived while I was in New York—I felt foolish. Did I make the whole thing up? Maybe I just wanted to believe God wanted me to build my business here. What if that wasn't the case at all?

For the next six weeks, I went into the office every day, believing something would pop up. In the meantime, I focused on writing and finding new potential clients. But the truth was, I was afraid I'd made a massive mistake. The office wasn't going to pay for itself.

One day, I decided it was time to have a conversation with God. But before I could talk to Him, I needed to get clear on what I wanted to say.

I walked up to my whiteboard and started writing:

- *Books, multiple.*
- *Clients. High-touch.*
- *Retreats (Camino?)*
- *Podcast? About what?*
- *Speaking.*
- *Serving. Always serving.*

After I finished writing, I sat on the floor and stared at the whiteboard, letting the ideas sink in. Then I closed my eyes and imagined: What would it feel like to publish multiple books? To sign them? To mentor clients? I pictured each dream in detail.

Once I was done, I thanked God for all my blessings and for helping me make these dreams come true. Placing my hand over my heart, I whispered, "God, I don't know how this will happen, but I trust You placed these ideas in my heart for a reason, and I trust You will show me the way. I just have to be patient."

I sat still, holding all the emotions I imagined I would feel when I had achieved everything I had written: pride, joy, gratitude, and a deep love for my purpose to help women.

And then the tears came. An overwhelming sense of peace filled me, and I began to sob. Each tear fell faster than the last, and soon, the top of my shirt was soaked. In that stillness, an image came to me: a group of women surrounded me, all singing Neil Diamond's "Sweet Caroline." When we got to the chorus, I changed the words. Instead of "Sweet Caroline," I belted out, "My Lord Divine." We all burst into laughter.

At that moment, sitting on the floor in front of the church, I couldn't help but chuckle. *God has quite a sense of humor.*

"Oh, God," I said, wiping away tears. "That's so good." Then it hit me—I had accidentally sung part of the song's chorus.

"So good, so good!" I repeated, laughing harder than I had in years. Soon, the room radiated an immense joy that surrounded me completely. And then, suddenly, I understood.

God had brought me close to Him. He had to give me an office to get my attention, to put me right where He wanted. And then He sat me down right before him, cross-legged like a child, and taught me a lesson. Just like He had brought me closer to Him now, He was charging me to bring others along, too.

"I don't know how to do that, God," I said aloud. "I don't know how."

But I didn't need to wait for Him to answer. I already knew—He would show me the way.

That day changed everything. I stepped away from the executive world and started focusing on what truly mattered to me: supporting women on their own journeys to God. All my earlier plans had been gently, lovingly redirected, guiding me back to the path I was always meant to walk.

REFLECTIONS

Reflect on an area in your life where you struggle to let go. What fears or beliefs might be holding you back from fully surrendering this to God?

How would your life look different if you fully trusted that God's plan is for your highest good, even when the path is unclear? What could you gain—or let go of—by embracing that trust?

Surrender often means setting aside our desires to align with God's will. How might you open yourself to see His hand in unexpected places, even in moments of disappointment or challenge?

Closing Reflections from Trisha

There are moments in life that change everything. For me, one of those moments happened twenty years ago, during the Christmas miracle that transformed my family. It wasn't just the snow—though seeing it blanket South Texas on Christmas Day was unforgettable. It was what the snow represented: hope restored, my dad's heart healed, and a second chance for our family.

But I didn't accept the miracle right away. While my parents' faith deepened, I wrestled with doubt and uncertainty. It's taken me years to fully embrace what happened that night and to understand how God was working not just in my dad's healing but in my own heart.

This year, celebrating my dad's 70th birthday felt like a reminder of just how far we've come. Twenty years after doctors told us he wouldn't live to see his 50s, my dad's heart is strong, and his faith is even stronger. He has served as a deacon for fifteen years, answering the call he felt during that snowy Christmas. My mom continues her work in ministry, inspiring others through her devotion and grace. Together, they've built a life that's a testament to the quiet, steady power of faith and prayer.

As for me, I've found my calling in helping others rediscover their faith and trust in God's plan. Through my work as a transformative life mentor and coach, I walk alongside women who are overcoming fear, loss, and doubt, guiding them toward the freedom that comes with

CLOSING REFLECTIONS FROM TRISHA

surrender. I've also had the joy of sharing conversations about faith with my parents through our podcast, *Bad Catholic*. It's a reminder that this journey is ongoing—for all of us—and that God continues to meet us exactly where we are.

As we end this journey together, my mom and I hope you've felt the quiet ways God moves in each of our lives. Maybe you saw glimpses of your own story reflected here—those moments of questioning, those small nudges and the unexpected people who crossed your path just when you needed them. We hope you've discovered that you're not alone in facing the unknowns, the setbacks, and the joys.

Through it all, one thing has become more apparent to me: God is always speaking to us, guiding us, and walking beside us. But His voice is often quiet, and we can easily miss it if we're not paying attention. In the book of Isaiah, we are reminded of God's guidance: *"Whether you turn to the right or to the left, your ears will hear a voice behind you, saying, 'This is the way; walk in it.'"* (Isaiah 30:21). Even when it feels like we're in the dark, His guidance is constant.

For years, Jeremiah 29:11 defined my life and guided me through my moments of doubt and uncertainty. I clung to it: *"For I know the plans I have for you," declares the Lord, "plans to prosper you and not to harm you, plans to give you hope and a future."* It held me steady when I felt lost, and I believed in God's promise. The other day, though, I found myself reading further and came upon Jeremiah 29:12-14 for the first time. And I wept. I realized that while I needed Jeremiah 29:11 in an earlier season of my life, God chose *this* moment to speak to me through the following words:

"Then you will call on me and come and pray to me, and I will listen to you. You will seek me and find me when you seek me with all your heart. I will be found by you," declares the Lord.

These words feel like an invitation and a reminder that the journey doesn't end with the promise of a plan—it continues in the pursuit of a relationship. I know this Scripture will define this chapter of my life as I seek Him with all my heart.

If you're going through a time of uncertainty, loss, or transition, know that these struggles are a meaningful part of your journey. God doesn't leave us to wander without purpose; instead, He uses these times to shape us, to call us back to Him. One of the simplest yet most transformative things we can do is take a moment to sit quietly with God. There's no need to overcomplicate it. Find a quiet space, close your eyes, and say, "Lord, I'm here. Show me the way."

I'd love for you to try this: commit to spending five minutes daily in quiet reflection or prayer. Start by thanking God for one small blessing from your day, then ask Him to show you where He's leading you. This practice may feel small, but it's a powerful step toward opening your heart and hearing God's gentle guidance.

As you move forward, remember that each step is part of a greater story. Trust that God's timing is perfect and that His promises are constant, even when He's drawing us into something more profound. When we learn to trust in that, even our quietest moments of faith become miracles.

Thank you for joining us on this journey. I pray that you leave with a little more peace, hope, and the confidence that, no matter where you are, God is already at work in your story. And now, as we each seek Him with all our hearts, may we find Him, always closer than we imagined.

XO,
Trish

Closing Reflections from Toni

As for prayers, I've learned that not all are answered the way we hope. Some of mine were answered; others were not. Those that went unanswered may not have been part of His plan or, perhaps, will be resolved at some future date.

Why did He answer some and not others? I'll never fully know, and I won't dare question His reasons. I'm just a tiny part of this vast world, yet somehow, God hears me. That is enough.

Walking with Christ is not easy; some days, I still want to crawl back into the dark places I've known. But choosing Him brings purpose and life. I was created to know Him, to serve Him, and to follow Him. "Pray without ceasing"—those words have a depth I never understood until I became a mother.

When my daughters left for college, I felt them slipping from my hands, beyond my guidance but never beyond my prayers. I prayed with every ounce of boldness I had, trusting God to watch over them, even when I couldn't see their faith growing.

There were times I had almost lost hope. But then, without warning, God moved in their lives in ways I could never have foreseen. Trisha, who once walked away from God, is now on her own journey of faith. She studies Scripture, shares her story, and championed the creation of this very book. God had a plan all along, working in her heart with patience and grace. Like the Prodigal Daughter, she has returned to a Father who welcomes her with open arms.

Lisa, too, is finding her path, led by a divine inner guidance that she honors and trusts. Her openness to God fills me with pride and love. She's made pilgrimages to holy sites, visiting Assisi and Medjugorje alongside Trisha, and this year, she plans to visit the Shrine of Our Lady of Guadalupe in Mexico City. I see in her an eagerness to explore her faith in her own way, guided by God's gentle voice. Her journey is unfolding, and I am filled with gratitude to see her finding peace through her faith.

And then there is David, my rock and my greatest partner in life. This year, we celebrated 50 years of marriage. From 19-year-olds with nothing but hope, we have been blessed with a life rich in God's love and grace. Together, we have shared so much—trials and blessings alike—and today, we serve our community side-by-side at Saint Monica's Catholic Church in San Antonio. When I look at the life we've built, the people we've been blessed to serve, and the joy of knowing that everyone we love is healthy, I am filled with gratitude for the abundance of God's love that sustains us.

So, I say to anyone who feels weary: pray without ceasing. Trust in God's time, even when His silence is hard to bear. Just as He ran to my daughters and sustained my marriage through its trials, He will draw near to you, welcoming you with open arms.

God Bless You,
Toni

For I know the plans I have for you," declares the Lord, "plans to prosper you and not to harm you, plans to give you hope and a future. Then you will call on me and come and pray to me, and I will listen to you. You will seek me and find me when you seek me with all your heart.

—JEREMIAH 29:11-13

ACKNOWLEDGEMENTS
from Trisha

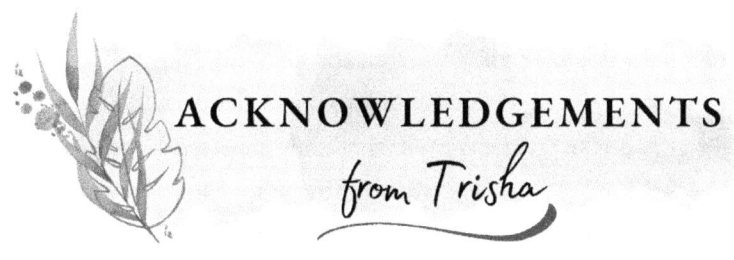

Bending Palms has been a lifetime in the making, even if we didn't always realize it. By God's grace, we have arrived at the time when we can share these stories with you.

Lord, thank You for calling on us; we hope we've made You proud.

To Dad and Lisa, you complete my family. Your unwavering support, commitment, patience, and love have been invaluable. Thank you for always being there for me.

To Mom, thank you for joining me in this project. I know it was a leap of faith. Your courage, honesty, and vulnerability will no doubt touch many lives. You've been a remarkable role model for Lisa and me, and we're grateful for all you've overcome—for yourself and for us. Our lives are richer and filled with more joy because of you.

To Grandma and Grandpa Espinoza, thank you for loving and caring for all of us for so long. You've left an everlasting mark on our family, and it's a blessing to be called your granddaughter.

To Grandma Fernandez, thank you for gifting me your love of music and perfume and for all the homemade tortillas—I can still taste them.

To all of our extended family, including those we've lost—thank you for the beautiful memories and legacy you left us. I love and cherish you all.

ACKNOWLEDGEMENTS

To my friends who stood by me, cried with me, and held me through hard times, thank you from the bottom of my heart. And to everyone who helped bring this book to life—friends who patiently listened to my dream (perhaps more than they expected!), those who encouraged my growth as a writer, and those who inspired me with their steadfast support—I am deeply grateful. Your role in this journey has been invaluable.

With love,
Trisha

I want to express my heartfelt gratitude to everyone who has supported me throughout this journey. To my family and all the friends who have walked with me in faith, your steadfast love will forever stay with me.

To my husband, David, and my daughters, Trisha and Lisa, thank you for your unwavering encouragement and understanding. Your love kept me motivated.

I especially want to thank my mother, Antonia. Her strength, courage, and love for her children often came with tough love. She instilled strong morals and values and ensured we had the foundation to survive in this world. Thank you, Mommy; you live in me and will forever be in my heart. You are my hero.

I'm also especially grateful to my God for the time I was given with my brothers, Joe and Emilio, and my beautiful sister, Gloria. Though they are no longer with us, they are alive in our hearts, and I will always cherish the conversations we shared about our love for Christ. I miss them so much, and I know they are cheering me on from above.

Lastly, I extend my deep appreciation to my daughter, Trisha. Your persistence, gentle nudges, and unwavering love for God gave me the courage to write down these stories and share how God is always in the midst of our lives.

I give God all the glory for nothing is impossible for Him!

Thank you for your love and support.

With all my love and prayers,
Toni

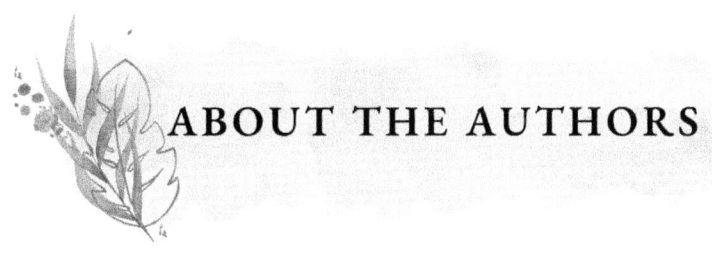

ABOUT THE AUTHORS

Trisha F. Espinoza is an ICF-certified life coach, executive development coach, and leadership expert whose mission is to inspire accomplished women to step boldly into the extraordinary lives God designed for them. A two-time award-winning media executive, Trisha has held leadership roles at global powerhouses like WarnerMedia, NBCUniversal, and Paramount. She has been recognized as one of the "Most Influential Minorities in Cable" and featured in *Deadline*, *Variety*, and *Texas Monthly*.

As a mentor and coach, Trisha has guided countless minority professionals to thrive in their industries and empowered women around the globe to overcome self-doubt, embrace divine purpose, and rewrite the narratives holding them back. She is a proud Texas State University graduate and holds a Cable Executive Management certificate from Harvard Business School's Executive Education program.

Trisha is the co-creator of the *Bad Catholic Podcast*, a space for those who identify as "bad Catholics" seeking to better understand and deepen their faith. Alongside her parents, Toni and Deacon David, Trisha shares relatable stories, asks honest questions about faith and explores how God works in everyday life with humor and authenticity.

Her forthcoming memoir is an unflinching look at the messy, beautiful process of healing and faith. Through raw storytelling, Trisha opens up about the personal battles that shaped her—from toxic rela-

ABOUT THE AUTHORS

tionships and career burnout to miscarriages and addiction. This memoir is a testament to the power of God's grace, told with wit, vulnerability, and a perspective only Trisha can deliver. Her story is for anyone who's ever felt broken, doubted miracles, or wondered if they could find their way back to faith.

LEARN MORE ABOUT TRISHA'S JOURNEY AND HER WORK AT TRISHAESPINOZA.COM.

Toni F. Espinoza has dedicated over four decades to faith formation and serving the Catholic community. Beginning her career in 1983 at Holy Spirit Preschool in McAllen, Texas, Toni quickly rose from teacher to director, a position she held for 25 years. During this time, she also led Youth Ministry for high school students, organizing retreats, fundraisers, conferences, and faith-building activities.

In 2006, Toni began her Spiritual Direction formation with the Archdiocese of San Antonio, committing to extensive travel from the Rio Grande Valley to pursue her calling. After relocating to San Antonio, she joined the Saint Monica Catholic Church staff in 2022 as the Director of Religious Education. In this role, she oversees Sacramental Programs for Reconciliation, First Communion, and Confirmation, guiding over 500 students from kindergarten through high school.

Toni's deep faith has led her on pilgrimages to some of the most sacred sites in the world, including Fatima, Lourdes, Assisi, Rome, and the Basilica of Our Lady of Guadalupe. She has a profound devotion to Padre Pio, whose lifelong suffering and misunderstood nature resonate deeply with her.

When she's not immersed in her ministry, Toni enjoys listening to music, reading, watching the birds in her garden, and cheering for the San Antonio Spurs. Her unwavering commitment to nurturing faith and her love for her community continue to inspire everyone she serves.

www.ingramcontent.com/pod-product-compliance
Lightning Source LLC
Chambersburg PA
CBHW060839050426
42453CB00008B/755